Just Get Up Out
of Your Seat

Just Get Up Out of Your Seat

Billy Graham

Catherine Mackenzie

CF4•K

I dedicate this book with thanks to my Mum and Dad. This book would never have been written without both of you! To my friends at the Bible Study who prompted me about my unfinished manuscript. And to the Kingsview Y.F. who agreed to watch the DVD with me and drink hot chocolate. You have all contributed to this publication.

10 9 8 7 6 5 4 3 2

Billy Graham: Just Get Up Out of Your Seat
© Copyright Catherine Mackenzie 2007
ISBN: 978-1-84550-095-5
Reprinted 2012
Published by Christian Focus Publications Ltd,
Geanies House, Fearn, Tain, Ross-shire
IV20 1TW, Scotland, UK.
Tel: 01862 871011 Fax: 01862 871699
www.christianfocus.com
email: info@christianfocus.com
Cover design by Daniel van Straaten
Cover illustration by Artistic License
Printed and bound by Nørhaven, Denmark

This is not a fictionalised biography though dialogue has been imagined by the author. This book is based on the life of Billy Graham and the following materials have been used as source materials alongside the Billy Graham Evangelistic Association website www.billygraham.org
DVD - Billy Graham God's Ambassador
BOOKS - *Just as I am* by Billy Graham; *To all the Nations: The Billy Graham Story* by John Pollock; *Billy Graham God's Ambassador* by Russ Busby; *Footprints of a Pilgrim* by Ruth Bell Graham.

'As I grow older, my confidence in the
inspiration and authority of the Bible has
grown even stronger.
So has my conviction that only Christ
can give us lasting hope.'
Billy Graham
August 14th 2006

RUTH BELL GRAHAM 1920-2007

Mrs. Ruth Bell Graham, beloved wife of the
evangelist Billy Graham, died at her home
in Little Piney Cove, Montreat, N.C.,
surrounded by her husband and all five
children. This book was completed by the
author prior to Ruth's death on
June 14th 2007.

Contents

When the Guns Fell Silent

The guns fell silent on the Western Front. The war that had set country against country and people at each other's throats had now burned itself out. The First World War was over. There was victor and vanquished, but there were countless graves which seemed to say that nobody had really won. The final bullet of the war to end all wars had been fired but the seeds for future conflict had been sown. A piece of paper was signed, a treaty was made. It would be called the Armistice; A state of peace ... a peace that wouldn't last. People desperate for this message of hope would find it disintegrating as the decades passed. However, four days after the Armistice was signed a woman who had been picking beans all day in the North Carolina soil felt the first twinges of labour pain. A child was born who would find another message of hope but not a new one. This child would proclaim a message as old as time itself... the message of a Saviour ... the message of Jesus Christ.

That child was Billy Graham. His Saviour is Jesus Christ and it is his message of hope that is the thread throughout this whole story.

'Yes sir! Take me to the Cross for I can find my home from there!'

Fancy Ties and Tarzan Games

The small town of Charlotte was relatively quiet until the town clock read thirty minutes after three. Then, as the school bell chimed and the doors to Sharon High opened, a throng of young people spilled out on to the streets. It was a typical day in a typical Southern American town, but two young men were chatting intensely as their classmates made last minute preparations for going home.

One was heard to complain, 'If I looked like Billy Graham I'd have a date every weekend too.'

The other youngster pushed himself back off the fence he'd been leaning on and sighed, 'Well, you may be right … but it's more than looks you know. He treats those girls real nice. He might be tall and blonde, but my sister says he's a gentleman.'

'Yes,' the other guy grimaced, 'He's got the looks alright. All the girls go for that blue-eyed boy and he's got all those fancy ties! A right ladies' man.'

'Come on! Not even you can call him that! He's really into base-ball and he's strong.'

'He's not exactly muscular though.' This guy was determined to be down on Billy.

'Skinny he may be but he gets up before dawn to go milking,' was the retort, 'just like any normal country boy. And then it's back to the farm straight after school to do it all again.'

'Yes,' agreed his friend, as he looked at the town clock's hand creeping on around the face. 'We should get going then, shouldn't we?'

'Yes, and there's the bus! It'll serve you right if you end up sitting next to Billy Graham after all that griping you've been doing. But knowing him he'll be sitting beside that girl who's just turned you down.'

With a scowl on one face, and a grin on the other the two boys made their way to the school bus.

Billy Graham was sitting at the back with some classmates beside him. There was not a girl to be seen anywhere. Almost every child on the bus that day was from one farm or other and they were all on their way home from school to pick up where they had left off in the morning. Farming families had a lot of chores to do, and there was always plenty of work. Everyone had to do their share. Billy Graham eventually got off the bus at Park Road, not much more than a little dirt lane surrounded by 200 acres of farmland. Peaceful hills were dotted with trees and cattle all round about. A picket fence or two, a corral and paddock could be seen in the distance. Some Jersey cows and calves grazed in the field. This was Billy Graham's home and he loved it. Waving goodbye to his friends, he was soon making his way down the farm track – away from the jealous eyes of one young man towards the smiling eyes of his mother, whose unusual Christian name was Morrow.

'Come on, Son. Reese is waiting for you over by the barn. There's plenty work to be doing.'

Billy grimaced, 'Back-breaking work, I'm sure,' he thought to himself. But there wasn't anyone else to do his chores, a guy had dignity. Even if the last thing in the world he wanted to do was farming, Billy had to do it. So he smiled at his mother and broke into an easy trot towards the barn.

Farming had been in the Graham family for generations, Billy remembered, as he rounded the corner and stopped for a second to scratch the ear of the family pet goat. As kids they had always been hitching some goat or other to a little cart. Billy and his sister Catherine had great times being pulled around the place. There were good things about living in the country. Farm life wasn't all that bad.

As he came up to the barn, fifteen-year-old Billy patted the flank of one of the cows that was batting her eyelashes at him from over the gatepost. 'We've got old Grandpa Graham to thank for the farm I reckon, even though folks call him a bit of a rogue. It's a good job that Dad and Uncle Clyde managed to pay off Grandpa's debts because now we've got a prosperous business.'

And that was certainly true. Holstein, Jersey and Guernsey cows made up a really good herd. All the hard work, which included getting up at three in the morning to milk, had definitely paid off. Billy looked along the field towards his family home. One of the best things about their new-found prosperity was the two-storey house they had been able to buy – and the fact that it had indoor plumbing. 'No more baths in a washtub on the back porch,' exclaimed Billy Graham. That was a big plus.

In the distance Billy spotted Reese Brown heading towards the barn. Earlier that day Reese had dehorned a bad-tempered young bull. Billy wished he'd seen it. Reese was the family's black foreman, an ex-army sergeant who had fought in the First World War. Billy looked up to the man with admiration. There wasn't anyone else he knew who could handle a difficult bull like Reese could. He was something else. Just then a dark brown hand ruffled Billy's hair, 'Hey Billy,' Reese smiled down at the young man. 'Going to help me today, son? Or are you just too rowdy and mischievous to be any use?'

Billy grinned. 'Yes sir, I mean, no, sir, I mean – I'm your man!'

Reese laughed out loud. 'You sure are! Come on, we've got a couple of Jersey cows to shift to the pasture over there and then my lovely wife has a whole stack of buttermilk biscuits all fresh from her oven just waiting for us.'

Billy let out a little whoop of joy. He knew his mother would say not to spoil his appetite, but with a growing boy like Billy Graham there was little danger of that. As his mother watched them through the kitchen window she turned towards her husband, who had come in from the farm, and sighed. 'I still say Billy Frank's got too much energy. That boy never runs down.'

Her husband looked up from what he was doing and nodded, 'That might be, Morrow. But just remember what the doctor said, "It's the way he's built." We must accept it and learn to live with it.'

Morrow Graham took another look at her son and the foreman handling the cows. 'He does all his work on the farm and still has time to play Tarzan in the woods.'

Mr Graham laughed, 'Do you hear all that yellin' and hollerin' he does. He frightens the wits out of the horses.'

Morrow giggled, 'Sure does. He's quite a prankster our son. Do you remember what he used to do to the bus driver?'

Mr Graham raised his eyes to the ceiling. 'Uh-huh. Good job the old man took it so good natured. Every afternoon, as our Billy Frank and his mates got off the bus, they'd reach underneath and turn off the valve to the gas tank. The engine would only go about a hundred yards before it would sputter out.'

Morrow laughed into her apron at the memory. 'What was worse was how that poor bus driver would get out to check what was wrong and there'd be Billy Frank jumping and skipping about, a big grin plastered all over his face. I suppose the driver had a good sense of humour or Billy Frank would have gotten in trouble for that.' Billy's mother wiped some crumbs off the sideboard, a warm smile on her face. 'Well, my son, – I wonder what God has planned for you.'

'I sure don't know the answer to that,' Mr Graham said, stretching out his legs before the stove. 'But if we leave the lad to his own devices he'll not do much more than baseball.'

'That's not true, dear,' Billy's mother protested. 'Why he just loves to read those history books of his.'

'Maybe. But if you were to ask him what the most important day of his life has been so far, he'd say, without a doubt, "The day I met Babe Ruth."'

'Well, Babe Ruth is the most famous baseball player this country has. Any boy would have been proud to meet him. All lads his age have big dreams and plans. I'd just ….You know …'

Mr Graham nodded his head in understanding. Both parents wanted to see their son show an interest in his spiritual life.

Mr Graham headed back out on to the farm once more. There was a lot to do before the evening meal and family devotions. 'Billy Frank never really strikes me as being that enthusiastic about the Bible. His mother and I'd just love to see that youngster turn to the Lord and love his ways. Maybe tonight he'll be more receptive when we read the scriptures.'

It's all Hogwash

Billy Graham was also thinking about family devotions. Leaving Mrs Brown's kitchen with another handful of buttermilk biscuits he was wondering about what it was that had changed his folks.

'It's strange. Can't quite put my finger on it,' Billy muttered to himself. 'We've always had family devotions. Mom and Dad have done that since the day they got married. But things have changed for sure. They're definitely more religious.'

Billy looked towards the kitchen window once more and nodded. 'Yeah, that's it. They seem to have gotten religion in a new way. I know we've always kept Sunday special and gone to church and sung Psalms and such like, but now things have really changed. I reckon Ma got it first. She went to that Bible Class with Auntie. But now Pa's got it too.'

Billy shivered. He was pretty sure he knew what had changed Mr Graham. One day, while working on the farm, a piece of wood had shot out from a mechanical saw and hit Billy's father straight on the head. It was such a serious injury that the surgeons believed that he would die. However, Billy's mother had mustered all her Christian friends to pray and then went up to her bedroom herself to kneel before the Lord and plead for the life of her husband.

Mr Graham had been a Christian believer for many years. As a young man he had come to love the Lord Jesus as his Saviour. But with the pressures of adult life and other such things his faith had lost its urgency and impact. He had still believed and brought up his family in a Christian way and so had no objections to his wife going to a women's Bible study meeting. Yet he wasn't that enthusiastic about worshipping the Lord. Farm work always kept him busy. There were bills to pay and times were hard financially in the 1930s. Even though the farm was prosperous, these days it was a hard job for any business to make ends meet. Then on top of all that came the accident. The last thing they needed - or maybe it was, in fact, the best thing that could have happened to Billy Graham's father.

On the day of the accident Mrs Graham had retreated to her room to pray and when she was finished she was absolutely certain that God had heard her.

Young Billy thought about this, carefully. 'Ma and Pa both believe that God spoke to them through that accident. Pa's made a full recovery – and I admit it – that's amazing. But now we all have to study the Bible and pray. They're even reading Christian books... which wouldn't be so bad if us kids didn't have to listen to them all the time too!'

With a snort and a bad-tempered kick at a dried up bit of cow manure Billy muttered to himself, 'It's all hogwash anyways and I'm not having anything to do with it.'

All of this change in the family religious life had taken place quite a few months before, and Billy saw no sign of it letting up. 'I reckon there's not a thing I can do about it,' he grumbled. 'I can't even complain. Pa would whip me for sure.' And that was true. There were just certain things that as a Graham family member you did and did not do.

You did go to church every Sunday. Not going was just not an option. In fact, if any of the Graham family had said that they weren't going to attend church, they'd have felt the sting of Mr Graham's belt or of Morrow Graham's long hickory switch. Discipline was part and parcel of growing up in that household.

You did live up to very high standards. Mr and Mrs Graham insisted that their young people lived a life of purity. You behaved and conducted yourself in a certain way. You were allowed out on dates but there was to be no drinking of beer or loose living with members of the opposite sex. You could have fun and friendship, and you were to be thankful for that. This sort of wise living made Billy a healthy, happy, good-looking, pleasant young man.

But this was as far as it had gone. The outside morality hadn't become a living inside faith. Billy did the right thing but his heart and mind were rebellious. His parents could see that, plain as day. Although their son kept his thoughts to himself about his 'religious' parents, a parent can pretty much tell when a teenager has no enthusiasm. Billy's parents knew that he had no inclination towards God or the church. Billy had no concern whatsoever for his soul.

As Billy kicked a clod into a pile of dust Morrow Graham comforted herself somewhat with the thought that her son's behaviour wasn't that bad. 'The worst he's done is almost wreck his father's car,' she sighed. 'That's pretty good going for a fifteen-year-old.' But as she reached across the stove to put another pot of vegetables on to boil she muttered anxiously to herself, 'What is he going to think of his father's plans? I suppose we'll know soon enough.'

That night Mr Graham was going to make an announcement just before family devotions. 'Billy won't say a word,' his mother reckoned. 'But I'll be able to read his thoughts.'

Just as I am?

'So this is what we plan to do,' Mr Graham announced to his young family that night after dinner. 'Thirty local businessmen want to devote a day of prayer to our town of Charlotte before the evangelistic campaign.'

'Evangelistic campaign?' one of the children queried.

'Yes. It's an eleven-week long series of meetings where people come along to hear the good news of Jesus Christ and how he died to save them from their sins.'

'Another church meeting?' Billy asked, slightly disgruntled.

'No son, in fact it's going to be nowhere near a church,' Mr Graham announced.

'You see,' his wife explained, 'The churches round about here aren't that keen on the idea. Mordecai Ham is coming to preach and some of the ministers don't seem to take to him that well, our one included.'

'So if it's not going to be in the church, where is it going to be?' Billy asked.

'Well, that's what I was going to say. The evangelistic meetings are going to be held in that specially made shelter in town. You know the place where Billy Sunday and those other revival preachers go. And we've agreed to let the businessmen use our pasture to set up a tent to hold their prayer meeting in. It seems they've got a burden for this town and they're going to bring it to the Lord. They want to see more spiritual life about this place and I've even heard one or two of the men mention how they want to pray for a preacher to come out of this area who will reach the world for Jesus. Big prayers for a little town. But, anyway, I'm behind these guys. So we're lending them the pasture – seems the least we could do. I'm not sure if we'll attend the evangelistic meetings in town. Haven't quite made up my mind about that.'

Billy nodded his head briefly and got back down to eating his mashed potatoes. Prayer meetings, evangelism… it was just more of the same. Ever since his parents had heard God speaking to them through his father's accident it was like they'd completely changed or something. 'Who would have thought you could get thirty businessmen together to pray about this place! That must mean there are another thirty men just as fired up as Ma and Pa? Gee Whiz! And if that's what they're like then Mordecai Ham must be off the scale. I can't believe he's going to be preaching here for eleven weeks!' Billy of course didn't say that out loud. That sort of talk was disrespectful and just asking for the sting of the hickory switch. But a fiery evangelist in town for eleven weeks! Billy wasn't the only one in Charlotte to think that this was taking religion too far.

Mordecai Ham was a renowned evangelist, someone who went around visiting different places telling people about Jesus and how they could have their sins forgiven. Mordecai Ham was also well known for putting preachers' noses out of joint. Some of the Charlotte preachers were already complaining. Mordecai Ham had been openly critical of the churches and the pastors of Charlotte.

'Sinful,' 'Unspiritual,' 'Cold,' and 'Complacent.'

Mordecai Ham was riled. Charlotte wasn't the godly church-going town it liked to pretend it was. The evangelist knew that this place was in need of a shake-up.

For the first few days of the evangelistic campaign Billy was relieved that his family showed no intention of going to the meetings. But then one day, as he returned from school to do the milking, a station-wagon was parked in the driveway. It was still there after milking was over so he entered the kitchen to see if he could find out who it was that was visiting.

There was no sign of his mother by the stove or in any of her other usual places, but her voice could be heard from the distant parlour. Billy spruced up a bit to prepare to meet with 'the company' and politely knocked on the door before entering. Mrs Graham was sitting on the settee with one of her neighbours who had just launched into an enthusiastic description of the Mordecai Ham evangelistic meetings.

'He's not afraid to skin those ministers,' the woman exclaimed. Billy's mother looked shocked at the expression. 'You see,' the visitor carried on, 'those pastors haven't been behind Mordecai's gospel preaching at all. The most powerful clergy in Charlotte oppose him. Even the newspapers are out for his blood. But that hasn't stopped him, no sir.'

She stopped for breath before continuing, 'His preaching is passionate and after I heard him I left that meeting knowing without a shadow of a doubt that Jesus Christ is alive! And this morning, when I heard that you Grahams hadn't been at any of the meetings, I thought, I am going to go straight over to that house and ask them all to come with us next time. And so I have. What do you say Morrow?'

'Well, thank you most kindly for asking us to come. That's right neighbourly of you, and as soon as my husband is in from the dairy I'll discuss it with him.'

'That's her told,' Billy thought to himself. But his thoughts were wrong as that evening over dinner Mrs Graham raised the subject with her husband. 'Do you think we should go?'

Mr Graham thought quietly for a moment or two. 'I think we should.'

Billy sighed deeply.

'I think we all should,' his father continued. 'But

it's quite a treck into town, and although I would like to see the kids attend I'll not force them. Billy's too old to be told to go to something like this.'

Relieved, Billy reckoned that he might just get out of going to this preaching shin-dig after all.

However, towards the end of the week something happened that changed his rather antagonistic behaviour. One morning as Billy arrived at Sharon High there was a furious discussion taking place in the school-yard. A gang of teenagers were huddled round one of the town newspapers. Billy overheard snippets being read aloud, 'Disgraceful conduct,' 'Shameful behaviour,' 'Fornication.'

Billy stopped in his tracks. 'Fornication,' he turned to look at the newspaper that was causing such a ruckus.

The article centred around one quote from Mordecai Ham's last night's sermon, where he had accused the local Charlotte teenagers of immoral living. Billy gave a low whistle. Fornication was a big word to describe sexual relations outside of marriage. That was quite an accusation for the prim and proper and supposedly upright Southern town.

The kids in school decided to do something about it. 'We're not going to stand here and let this Ham man say that kind of thing about us!' they declared. 'Let's go and tell him to his face what *we* think of *him*!' And with that a mass march was planned. Billy wasn't having anything to do with it but other teenagers decided to march right up to the evangelistic meeting to protest at the accusations. One good thing about all this fury was that Billy Graham began to think that perhaps a visit to a Mordecai Ham meeting might be more interesting than he had at first thought. What clinched it for him was a chat he had later on that night with Albert McMakin a local sharecropper.

'Come on Billy,' the young man urged. 'This preacher's not a sissy. Man, he's got fire in his belly. He's something else. I wouldn't be asking you to come unless I thought you just gotta hear this guy. I've got a whole truck load of people from the neighbourhood going to hear him - whites and blacks - hey, I'll even let you behind the wheel. How about it?'

Billy didn't need to think twice. Any excuse to sit behind the wheel of a motor vehicle!

And that was how the young Billy Graham attended his first evangelistic meeting, and it was one he would never forget.

Sitting at the back of the congregation, Billy and the others from Albert's truck looked out on one of the largest crowds of people that Billy had ever seen. Mordecai bounced up on to the platform and began to preach with his usual famous brand of fire and vigour. Billy was spellbound.

'Man, this guy can preach!' he thought to himself. Then moments later Billy gulped self-consciously. 'How does he know about that?' he found himself thinking. Mordecai Ham had exactly described a particular sin that Billy himself had a problem with. 'That's kind of embarrassing how he can describe all those sins of mine. I could be in trouble here,' Billy worried as he heard more about his sin and the very real divine judgement that he deserved. 'This preacher is telling me that I've got to mend my ways. But it's not as though I'm that bad really.'

Over the next couple of weeks that was the way things went for Billy back and fore to the Mordecai Ham meetings. Nothing could keep him away. Then it was back and fore with his thoughts too. At first it was, 'I'm a sinner.' Then it was, 'But I'm not that bad.' Then it would be back to, 'I'm in danger of being punished for my sin.' Then Billy would argue, 'I'm not like those other kids.' If he caught himself thinking, 'I've got to mend my ways,' he'd disagree with his own mind and say, 'but my ways don't need that much mending. I'm doing OK.'

***

Billy's sixteenth birthday came and went, and that was when his friend Albert began to notice a change in the teenager. 'Something's up,' he thought, as he looked across at Billy behind the wheel of the farm truck. 'He's kind of losing something. Doesn't have that smarty-pants, I'm alright, church-boy look about him any more... and that might be a good thing.'

And it was. Billy Graham had been brought up in a Christian home, had gone to church for as long as he could remember, knew all the Bible stories and was part of a town that considered itself very upright and God-fearing. However, the truth of the matter was that going to church and doing all the 'Christian' things wasn't real faith. These were just things that people did, and unless the people who did them had a real relationship with Jesus Christ they meant nothing. Up to that point Billy had gone through his life thinking that if he was going to church like a good boy, obeying his parents, being an upright and moral citizen then he didn't really need to think too much about what would happen when he died. However, Mordecai Ham's preaching was changing all that.

Every time he went to a meeting Billy felt as though the long-fingered preacher was pointing right at him. Billy would hope that some woman with a big hat would sit in front of him. At least that way he'd be able to hide from the preacher's accusing finger. But even when that happened it didn't do any good, Mordecai still seemed to be able to get round whatever head gear was being worn and point straight at Billy. The only thing to do was to join the choir. They were looking for members, but they must have been desperate as it was a well-known fact that Billy Graham couldn't sing a note, far less carry a tune. But join the choir he must, because they sat up at the back behind the preacher. So Billy sang tunelessly, while struggling with severe guilt over his sin. In the end his change of seating arrangements didn't help at all.

He might not be facing the preacher any more but he was still facing his need of salvation. The more he tried to convince himself that he was doing OK the more Billy felt the weight of his sin and how truly lost he was without Christ.

In the space of a few short weeks Billy had gone from being a young lad who was sure he had nothing to fear for his soul, to being broken in his spirit and longing to be saved from eternal judgement. He'd come to realise that his so-called 'upright' life wasn't enough. Billy had to give himself to Christ with nothing held back. Mordecai Ham preached about how God was willing to take the burden of sin away from anyone who would give their life to Jesus. All he had to do was to give his life to Christ and Christ would be his Saviour and his Friend.

As Mordecai Ham continued to preach on the way of salvation, night after night Billy Graham slowly focused less on the evangelist and more upon the One of whom the evangelist was speaking – Jesus Christ. But even then the sixteen-year-old was not willing to give up his life. Christ would have to become his master and this was a price that Billy was not willing to pay. He knew he was a sinner. He knew he needed Christ. He knew for a fact that Jesus was alive, but he knew that he wasn't going to give in... not yet.

A young cousin happened to be on hand one day when Billy was particularly concerned about what was going on in his life.

'You should go forward,' the boy told Billy.

Billy wondered. It was what a lot of the people at the meetings had been doing. At the end of every service Mordecai gave what he called an 'altar call.' It was a point in the service where you would walk down the sawdust path between the seats at the meeting hall in order to talk with someone at the front.

Billy didn't sing in the choir that night, instead he sat as near to the front of the congregation as possible. Mordecai Ham's face seemed just feet away from him, and when he heard the verse, 'God commendeth his love toward us in that while we were yet sinners, Christ died for us,' Billy thought that Mordecai must have said that verse especially for him. He knew he was a sinner, he knew that Christ had come to save him, but he was still struggling. Did Jesus really want to save him, a sinner, reluctant to be saved, unresponsive to the love of Christ, someone who was still holding on to his life, unwilling to give anything to the one who had died for him on the cross?

The verse told Billy Graham that, yes, God loved him. He loved him while he was still a sinner. Christ had died for him while he was still a sinner. And Billy Graham must go forward and tell the world that he believed and would give his life to the Lord.

Still he struggled. The choir sang hymns as men and women and young people made their way forward, but Billy remained in his seat. He remained in his seat through every one of the verses of 'Just as I am without one plea.' But when the next hymn was sung Billy Graham got up out of his seat and made his way to the front. He could stand it no longer; he had to commit. As he moved down to the front of the podium his parents breathed a sigh of relief. It was the answer to fervent and anxious prayers. Billy's father waited for a bit before running down to the front after his son to give him a great big hug.

That night Billy Graham sat on the edge of his bed. A typical teenager, son, a brother, a young man in a hurry you might say. It had been a long and painful process for him to give in and give his life to Christ. 'I hope I stick it out,' he muttered to himself as he ducked underneath the covers.

Preacher Boy

'Well, son,' Mr Graham said a couple of years later. 'You're eighteen now and more than ready for college. But we'll miss you when you're gone. Tennessee didn't work out for you but your mother and I think that the Florida Bible Institute will be much better. The climate will be warmer for a start.'

Morrow Graham nodded her head vigorously. 'Yes. You caught the flu twice during the Christmas vacation and your breathing still isn't quite right. I think it's the right decision to change college, really I do.'

Billy nodded, relieved that his parents supported his decision not to go back to Tennessee. He just hadn't been happy there after leaving high school. The college hadn't suited him – and neither had the climate. Feeling sick because of his repeated bouts of flu Billy had visited the family physician who prescribed sunshine. This was something Tennessee didn't really have a lot of, but Florida had it in truckloads. So Billy left North Carolina for the State of Florida to go to Bible college and then on to other things.

But first things first, he had to get to know his fellow students. That wasn't too hard.

***

'Billy's a good fellow to have around,' a class-mate exclaimed one afternoon after lessons were over. 'I'm looking forward to seeing what kind of snazzy bow-tie he'll wear tonight. He's got such a collection!'

Another classmate giggled as she pictured the energetic young man. 'He's fun and no mistake. Everything he does, he does with such energy. When we were washing dishes the other day in the kitchens, Billy boasted that he could wash dishes fast enough to keep four girls busy drying. Well, we put that to the test! And he could!'

'I heard him talking about how he first gave his testimony at a small county jail to the inmates and guards. That's quite something, I reckon. The other week I came across him telling people about the Lord Jesus outside the dog track at Sulphur Springs.'

'But preaching in front of a congregation, that's entirely different,' the young girl interrupted.

'Yes, you're right,' her friend agreed. 'It's just as well the Dean didn't give Billy a chance to say no. He would never have agreed to preach if he'd had prior warning.'

As it turned out Billy Graham hadn't been at the Florida Bible Institute for a year before he was 'persuaded' to preach his first sermon. It had all started when Billy was asked by the head or Dean of the college, Mr Minder, to spend his Easter vacation with him near Lake Swan in Northern Florida. Billy agreed and, on Easter Sunday, he'd got into the car with Dean Minder. Their first port of call was Palatka where Minder's friend, Cecil Underwood, was working as a Baptist preacher. On their arrival they discovered Underwood was trying to arrange a preacher to give a sermon at the Bostick Church, that evening. 'Could you do it for me?' Underwood asked Mr Minder. 'No, but Billy will,' was Minder's quick response.

Billy's protests that he had never preached before, and couldn't do it now, fell on deaf ears.

'You're preaching tonight,' Mr Minder explained. 'And when you run out of steam I'll take over.'

When they arrived at the church Billy walked up to the pulpit and looked out on to a congregation of about thirty cowboys and ranchers, accompanied by an assortment of dogs, scratching and sniffing around their masters leather boots. Sick to the stomach and sweating uncomfortably Billy began his address and eight minutes later completed it.

However, that night the pastor who had arranged the evening, noted one thing about Billy Graham – his sincerity. Cecil Underwood didn't mind that the young man had gone in and out of the pulpit in under ten minutes because he'd said what he'd said out of real conviction. Billy had meant every word. He believed what he preached, absolutely.

Billy's classmates were probably right about the young preacher. He might never have agreed to do it if he'd been given a chance to think over things. What his classmates didn't know at that point was how often their friend would preach in the future.

The next time he preached, however, Billy was still terrified. He felt totally inadequate and unprepared. Again, Dean Minder had asked him to preach a sermon. This time it was going to be to the young people at the Dean's church and there wouldn't be a cowboy or a hound-dog in sight. Billy was nervous to say the least, so nervous that he decided he was in dire need of some practice.

'It's the only way I'm going to get over these jitters,' he admonished himself, as he stepped up on a tree stump in the middle of the woods. Taking a deep breath he launched into his 'practice sermon' – his 'congregation' being a rather startled bunch of rabbits and squirrels. The animals scampered into the bushes as Billy's voice grew more confident. They certainly didn't pay much heed to the message. But the youngsters at the Tampa Gospel Tabernacle were much more receptive. They enjoyed hearing someone their own age preach with such energy and force.

'You've been called to preach,' was what Brunette Brock, the college secretary said to Billy. 'God is calling you to preach his word.'

But Billy wasn't sure. He had doubts about whether he was able to be a real preacher.

'I'm not educated enough. Yes, I've been through high school and I'm at Bible College, but other than that I don't think my education is really up to scratch. I'm just not cut out to be a preacher.' But even then Billy still felt a strong inner urge to do just that – to preach.

He knew that men like Dean Minder and other prominent evangelical preachers were concerned about how the country of America was losing its way. What they meant was that America was turning away from God. Church buildings were emptying, religion was on the decline, America needed to have someone to call it back to God.

As well as this Billy was certain that his own Christian life had to be serious; it had to be meaningful. He knew that if he kept going the way he had done over the last few years he could very well drift away from Christ and end up a spiritually-ineffective Christian, bringing harm to the name of Christ rather than being a powerful witness for the Lord.

His desire to see himself completely given over to Christ, and to see his country called back to God, were two of the things that eventually changed Billy from being a young man uncertain about what he was supposed to do, to being a man of purpose and conviction, sure in his calling from God. Another upheaval in Billy's life reinforced this.

***

It wasn't a surprise that the handsome young man from North Carolina soon had a pretty girl on his arm, and that girl was wearing his engagement ring. Emily Cavanaugh was just one year older than him and was a delightful companion for any young man about town. She sparkled in company, and was a great girl to have in a conversation because of her vivacious character and intelligence. Billy was in love from the first moment he saw her and soon proposed marriage. She accepted. But they hadn't been engaged a year before Emily began to have doubts and asked Billy to pray about whether or not they should continue with their engagement.

Billy agreed, and for fifteen minutes every day he focused on praying to God that they should get married, but only if it were God's will. This focus on prayer in Billy's life was of great benefit to him. He had never really prayed like that before; he'd never had such a specific need. Billy's prayers were answered, but not in the way you might think.

The most important night of the student calendar was fast approaching. Class night was the ultimate social occasion for the college in which there were many young people and courting couples. Each young man fortunate to have a date accompany him would buy his girl a corsage of flowers to pin to her dress.

Two boys bought a corsage for Emily Cavanaugh. Billy Graham was one of them. But Emily didn't wear his corsage.

During the evening she quietly came up to Billy and asked to speak to him in private. The young girl had slowly, but surely, fallen in love with another of Billy's classmates, a young man he admired and respected.

'Billy,' she whispered anxiously. 'I've agreed to marry Charles. I'm sorry.' And with that, sitting together on a swing, the two young people agreed to part as friends. However, Billy's heart was broken. As Emily disappeared to rejoin the social gathering he looked around to see if there was anyone he could turn to in his trouble.

Dean Minder caught his eye and he made his way over. When Billy shared his sadness with his mentor and teacher the older Christian did a very wise thing and soothed the young man's aching heart with a word from the Bible. 'The God of all comfort comforteth us in all our tribulation, that we may be able to comfort them which are in any trouble.' With that Billy took a deep breath and rejoined the others at the party.

As he re-entered the throng of celebrating students Billy decided that what had happened was not going to make him bitter and resentful. Instead, he was going to let God do what was necessary with his life, even if meant bringing heartbreak into it.

And it was at that point that Billy really accepted that God had, in fact, called him to be a preacher. It was time for the young man to grow up and get serious about his study and about preaching God's Word.

Ask Her for a Date!

'Ouch, that hurt,' Billy Graham sat on the edge of the pavement, gently massaging his aching joints. He'd just been rather ungraciously flung out of a bar for preaching the gospel. 'Did he have to be so violent?' he complained. Billy stroked his stiff shoulder. The bar-tender had shoved him out the door of the Franklin Street Bar where the young preacher had promptly tumbled into a heap on the pavement outside.

'He did tell you to leave and you refused,' another student pointed out.

Billy groaned as someone tried to help him get up off the pavement. He had begun his preaching career in earnest. Instead of waiting around for people like Dean Minder to ask him to take a service, he was now creating his own opportunities to share the good news of Jesus Christ. On street corners, in front of bars and saloons, the young man would preach to the people on the very worst streets of Tampa, Florida.

Billy sighed as he heaved himself up into a standing position and hobbled back to the campus with his fellow students. Maybe the next time would be easier, maybe it wouldn't. But each preaching experience was different from the last one and different again from the next. This was simply because Billy preached in such a variety of different places.

One Bible institute contact asked for a couple of young preachers to come and give an address at their church. Billy and another student attended. However, during the morning service they felt that things weren't going well.

'Something's missing,' Billy thought.

So that afternoon the two young men got down on their knees and prayed for hours on the dirt floor of a church member's garage. During the afternoon other church members were out on the streets drumming up support for the meetings. When Billy got into the pulpit in the evening not a seat in the place was empty. The building was filled to capacity with people wanting to hear what this young preacher had to say. But Billy still thought that things weren't right. He got to the end of his sermon and decided that he'd fluffed it. But when he told the congregation that those who wanted to could come to the front of the church to be prayed for, and to ask the Lord Jesus into their lives, thirty-two young people did exactly that. One person in particular that evening looked at Billy Graham and remarked, 'There's a young man who is going to be known around the world!'

It didn't seem to matter that he was loud. It didn't seem to matter that every time he preached his words came out fast and furious. You had to really watch or you might miss something. He even earned himself a nick-name – The Preaching Windmill. But people knew what he was talking about when he preached. The folks in the trailer-parks and bars, the tramps and alcoholics all understood this young man when he preached about the living Christ.

That year a female student from Florida Bible Institute spoke at the graduation ceremony. Maybe people didn't realise it then, but years afterwards friends and colleagues of Billy Graham looked back on her graduation address and saw a link between it and a young man who was soon to graduate from the same institution.

'At each critical epoch of the church,' she said, 'God has a chosen instrument to shine forth his light in the darkness. Men like Luther, John and Charles Wesley, Moody and others, who were ordinary men, but men who heard the voice of God … It has been said that Luther revolutionized the world. It was not he, but Christ working through him. The time is ripe for another Luther, Wesley, Moody. There is room for another name in this list.'

Whose names would be on that list was perhaps the question that some left the graduation ceremony with. One name would be that of Billy Graham. But it was a name that wouldn't be there on its own.

***

Ruth McCue Bell was a second year student at Wheaton College in Chicago. The year was 1940 and she was standing on the steps at East Blanchard Hall some time in the fall when a young man, six-foot-two or thereabouts, and with a shock of blonde hair rushed past her. 'There's a young man who knows where he's going!' she said to herself.

And it seems that that was exactly what Billy was. Twenty-one years old and already an ordained Baptist pastor his clear blue eyes burned with certainty that few young men of his age possessed.

But what had brought the young Billy Graham back to the northern states? The fact was that he had finally been given the chance of a university education and had leapt at the opportunity.

Later that week Ruth was outside a classroom where an early morning prayer meeting was being held. A voice rang out, clear and loud, a voice in prayer. It was a new voice, a voice she hadn't heard before. 'Now there is a man who knows to whom he is speaking,' she thought.

And though she hadn't met Billy Graham, when they were finally introduced outside the halls of residence she recognised the man and the voice – a man on whom she had heard 'God's hand seemed to rest.'

Billy had quite a reputation to live up to, but he wasn't thinking about any of that when he met with Ruth. For the second time in his life Billy Graham had fallen in love at first sight. This was the girl that all the guys had been talking about, the gorgeous girl he had seen just the other day walking across campus. She was the girl that everyone said got up at four in the morning for prayer. He'd heard about her, even thought longingly about her. 'What a wonderful person she must be,' he'd decided. And now here she was, face-to-face with him, the woman his mind had already been building up to extremely high virtue.

'Ask her for a date,' a friend whispered. But Billy, scared out of his wits, couldn't utter a word. Later in the study hall he finally managed to pluck up the courage to ask Ruth McCue Bell to accompany him to a rendition of Handel's Messiah. Billy waited on tenterhooks for her answer. Ruth calmly turned her head to look at him and said, 'Yes.'

So the following Sunday, amidst a flurry of snow, the two young Christians were seen going arm in arm to the concert. Prior to the date Ruth was in the usual panic, agonising over what to wear. Her choice was in fact rather limited; one home-made dress or another home-made dress. The daughter of overseas missionaries didn't have a lot of extra money to spend on clothes. But she was used to making do with very little, and the fact that she only had two dresses to call her own hadn't caused her any problems with getting dates in the past. In fact, her sister had counted a list of fifty-two different men that Ruth dated throughout her college days. In contrast, during his college years Billy Graham had dated no more than two young women.

When writing home to his mother Billy gushed about his new passion being so beautiful and sweet and the girl he was going to marry. There was no doubt that Billy Graham was love-struck.

Ruth, however, didn't really feel the same way. Towards the end of their first date Billy made an attempt to hold her hand and was clearly rebuffed. Dejected, he escorted her to the door of the women's dorms certain that he'd got absolutely nowhere with this particular campus gem. But in actual fact Ruth's heart, though not in love with Billy, was stirred enough to make her turn to God in prayer about the situation. That very Sunday night, as the notes of the Messiah twirled around in her head, she knelt beside her bed and said to the Lord, 'If I could spend the rest of my life serving you with Bill[1], I would consider it the greatest privilege imaginable.' For a young girl who had always insisted that she would end her days as a single female missionary, this in itself was quite a change of heart.

However, as Ruth wondered in a rather confused fashion about becoming either a wife or a missionary, Billy went around the college bemoaning the fact that he didn't stand a chance with such a beautiful, accomplished and spiritual young girl. He certainly had a very high opinion of her. And he was right to be that way. Ruth was attractive and very beautiful. Not

---

[1] Ruth Graham is one of two people who call Billy Graham Bill instead of Billy. Ruth has called him Bill throughout their entire relationship.

only that, she had a charming nature and character, one that was fun as well as being deeply spiritual. In fact, almost everything about Ruth was a pleasure to the people who knew her. She was courteous, intelligent and passionate about Christ. But on top of all that she had a delightful streak of mischievous fun which made her all the more real and a joy to be with.

So, it was little wonder that Ruth Bell was quite a sought after young woman – and that made Billy Graham even more disheartened. 'There's nothing that can possibly make her attracted to me,' he sighed.

But Ruth looked beyond the gangly country lad to see the man that he was becoming. He knew God, he had a purpose, he was dedicated. He wanted to please the Lord more than any man that Ruth had ever met. She also wanted to please God. But what would that involve? Could it possibly mean marriage to Billy? She wasn't sure – simply because for many years she felt that God was calling her to be a missionary. Since her early teens she had felt certain that her future life would be in Tibet. Her parents had left the State of Virginia in the U.S. for China to work as medical missionaries so Ruth had grown up as a missionary kid.

As a young woman on the brink of her further education in the United States Ruth had complained emphatically to her parents that she didn't need to go back to America in order to fulfil her calling. 'All I need is a working knowledge of the Tibetan language and a Bible.' But her parents, wisely, knew what was best for their young daughter. They insisted that she get on board the *USS McKinley* to cross the Pacific Ocean to the land of their birth.

It had not been the land of Ruth's birth, however, as her parents had been missionaries in China and Ruth had been born and brought up there. Nelson Bell, her father, was a missionary doctor and had spent years caring for the physical and spiritual needs of the people of that great land. Something of her parents' missionary zeal and passion seeped into Ruth's consciousness and she was convinced that the single missionary life was for her. Growing up amidst the civil war in China had not put Ruth off living as a frontier missionary. Bandits, gunfire in the night, air raids and kidnappings had all been part of her life in China, and China had been her home.

Ruth had also lived in North Korea for a while. At thirteen she had had to leave China to go to the PyengYang Foreign School. Desperately not wanting to go, Ruth had in fact prayed that God would permit her to die before she got on the boat. Thankfully God did not grant that request. And over the years that followed she went through school and eventually on to college in the United States, with her plans still set on being a single female missionary in Tibet. Now she was in her second year at Wheaton and it seemed as though her heart was being pulled equally in two directions. The once confirmed spinster was beginning to waver, but the confirmed missionary still held strong.

Billy Graham's name appeared frequently in Ruth's journal. She wrote poetry about the young man who even featured in her letters home. But their relationship didn't really go anywhere.

What effect was all this having on Ruth? Though she hadn't really admitted to being in love with Billy, her grades definitely began to suffer and she flunked one or two of her exams. Then Billy asked her out on another date – to hear him preach. No ball games or picnics for this young girl. She was, after all, dating Billy Graham – a young man in a hurry who knew exactly where he was going. She had noticed that about him on their first encounter and now she was experiencing it at first hand.

As they returned to Campus that evening Ruth noted his profile as he drove them through the Chicago traffic. The steel blue eyes reflected the lights of the cars that passed them in the night. And then as he walked her to her door his grip tightened on her arm, 'There is something that I would like you to make a matter of prayer. I have been taking you out because since the day we were introduced last fall I have been interested in you, more than interested. But I know that you have been called to the mission field.'

And there it was – their problem. Dates came and went but their problem always hung in the air between them. Their dilemma was still there even when Billy gave Ruth a ring to wear on her finger; an engagement ring. Yet even with that commitment the young couple still had difficulties to face. Ruth still stood by the belief that she had been called to Tibet, and therefore anyone that she was going to marry must be willing to go there too.

Several weeks passed and then came the ultimatum. 'Do you believe that God has brought us together?' Billy asked Ruth.

'Yes, I do,' she replied.

'Then,' Billy answered firmly, 'God will lead me, and you will do the following.'

If he hadn't said it in such a gentle and loving way Ruth might have been tempted to throw his ring back in his face. However, the man she had grown to know and love brought her to the realisation that following was precisely what she had to do.

Despite her reluctance Ruth agreed, there and then, to spend her life with Billy. The choice was clear even if it was difficult. She wanted to be an overseas missionary, but Billy had not been called by God to do that work. Ruth wanted to remain a Presbyterian, but Billy was a Baptist pastor. The ring was on her finger pointing her in the decision she would have to take. If Ruth felt she had to marry someone who was willing to go to Tibet then she would have to give

Billy back his ring, or let him take it off her. There was no way she would let that happen. Her missionary calling changed there and then. It didn't disappear, however. Instead God called her to be the helper and supporter of a young man who knew exactly where he was going and who knew the God he was going there with. Now Ruth was going too.

It would be a life of hard work and long separations. She knew that her new husband would have an increasing burden to bring lost souls to Jesus Christ. There would be a lot of work for him to do, increasingly active work. And Ruth would have to learn to blend into the background, her life quickly but necessarily disappearing into Billy's. Ruth would follow. Billy would lead. The Lord Jesus Christ would lead them both.

The Modesto Manifesto

The wedding took place not long after their graduation from Wheaton on Friday August 13th 1943. Ruth's parents had settled in the town of Montreat, in the mountains of North Carolina, when the political climate in China had hampered their return after furlough. This was where the wedding ceremony took place and Ruth was a typical young bride in many ways, anxious about her dress, and looking glorious. Unable to purchase a store bought wedding gown she had made her own wedding clothes with the help of a local seamstress. On the way to the church that morning, in order to preserve the perfect smoothness of her dress, Ruth insisted on standing as straight as she could in the back of her father's car. This way, as she walked down the aisle, she could be certain that her wedding gown was wrinkle free and looking splendid.

Billy only had eyes for her. This was the woman that God had been preparing for him. She was part of the almighty Creator's plan for Billy Graham's life. She was a woman who would stand beside her husband, dedicated to him and to his work, which after their seventy-five dollar honeymoon at Blowing Rock, would take them to a church in Illinois.

As they settled into their new life together Ruth became increasingly convinced that working as a full-time pastor was not what her young husband had been called to do. More and more she was certain that Billy was meant to be an evangelist, someone who would receive invitations to preach the gospel at a variety of places. This was a job for someone who had the common touch, who could communicate with ordinary men and women outside the church. Yes, pastors were important. They encouraged believers in Jesus Christ to learn from God's word and to share the good news of Jesus Christ with their friends and families. But evangelists were called to go straight to the unchurched people. Evangelists were called by God to preach, but not necessarily in church buildings. And Ruth knew that that was what Billy did best. At dog tracks, in bars, outside on noisy streets. Billy could preach anywhere.

Billy's new congregation was delighted with this energetic young preacher. His gifting for evangelism helped increase church attendance at Village Baptist Church in Western Springs, Illinois. House-to-house calls were organised to encourage the local community to come to hear Billy preach. Soon he launched a men's club for the business-men of the area, and before too long there were over three hundred men coming to hear an evangelistic talk every month. But Billy wasn't stopping there.

One evening in Northern Carolina an elderly

couple nipped out the back of their house and got themselves comfortable in their station wagon. 'Frank, turn up the volume loud enough for me to hear,' Morrow Graham instructed her husband.

'Soon as I get the station on this old radio,' the dairy farmer muttered. 'If that radio in the kitchen worked properly we could sit comfortably by the stove to listen to Billy. But it just won't pick up that station from Chicago.'

'Well, dear, don't you worry. A car isn't such a bad place to listen to your son broadcast on WCFL Radio.' The last part of the sentence was almost said in a gasp. Morrow Graham couldn't quite believe that it was their young Billy Frank speaking across the air waves, that he was a real live radio presenter. And as Mr Graham eased himself back into the driver's seat he and his wife spent a contented forty-five minutes listening to their son present *Songs in the night*, broadcast live from his church in Illinois. At 11 p.m., Frank reached over to turn off the radio until next week when the service would be broadcast yet again from their son's new church.

'I like that George Beverly Shea,' Morrow sighed. 'He sings real good.'

'Uh-huh, the young people like him too,' Frank agreed. 'Billy says that as soon as their own church services are over they hurry over to hear that guy sing,'

'Must be famous then?' Morrow asked.

'Guess so,' Frank agreed. 'He wrote that hymn "I'd rather have Jesus." All his own work that was. Billy just had to have him on his radio programme. Folks said to Billy that he'd never get that Bev Shea guy on his show. But Billy wouldn't listen, no Sir. He went to get an interview with the guy but the secretary said he was busy. When he was going out the door he noticed Bev Shea through this glass door and just went straight up to him. Asked him outright, there and then, if he wanted to come on his radio show. Now Bev Shea has got a regular spot on Songs in the Night. Good thing too seeing Billy can't sing,' Frank smiled as he shut the car door behind him and he and his wife headed off to their beds.

***

Billy's broadcasting opportunities helped him to focus on a variety of things. He deliberately worked on his Southern accent and softened it slightly. When you were broadcasting across the whole of the United States you had to be sure that people from New York understood you as well as the people in Alabama. He worked on his style. Alongside news and comments about world events he always gave an urgent gospel message, focusing on the listener's need to make an immediate decision for Christ. It was because of this, and Billy's instinctive understanding of young people, that he was chosen to speak at an exciting new event in the Spring of 1944.

Two men, Torrey Johnson and George Wilson had set up a special rally for young people in the Chicago area. It was going to be used to reach out to the young men of the services too. 'You see there are just so many of these young army and navy guys coming into Chicago on the weekends. If we get these youngsters having some good clean fun,' George explained, 'and we entertain them in a godly way, then we'll be able to share the good news of Jesus Christ with them too.' That was how Youth for Christ was formed in Chicago, and Billy Graham was asked to speak at their first event. It was the beginning of something big for the young preacher. An audience of 2,800 waited to hear him speak at the Orchestra Hall, a venue specially booked for the occasion.

A few months later Billy and Torrey Johnson met up in Florida while Billy was recovering after a doze of the mumps. Torrey outlined his plans for Youth for Christ: co-ordinated Saturday night rallies across the country, inspiring the American youth, finding a full-time organizer and evangelist for the organisation. And that evangelist was Billy Graham.

***

Ruth had always thought that Billy's calling was to be an evangelist. She knew this was right, but it wasn't easy for the young wife and mother as she cradled their first child. Little 'Gigi' had been born in September 1945. Gigi was short for Virginia, but was also the Chinese word for little sister, and her mother declared that she had been born with the biggest eyes that Ruth had ever seen in a baby. From the safety of her little bassinette, trimmed with Ruth's wedding veil, Gigi would just stare and stare at the world around her. Her father was the typical proud papa and would have just loved to have spent his life staring back at her.

In addition to parenthood life had changed dramatically in other ways. Accepting the new post at Youth for Christ meant that Billy had to hand in his notice to the church in Illinois. Then the Grahams had to head south again to set up a base near Ruth's parents in Montreat. They had a few pots and pans, but not a stick of furniture to call their own. Ruth, in fact, had to move in for a time with her parents, while Billy began what would be a life time of travelling.

Then he travelled across the United States and Canada. The time would come later for worldwide travel. For now it was America that Billy focused on and it was Montreat where Ruth would bring up their family and keep the home fires burning, supporting Billy in between his meetings and campaigns. It was there that she would also have some support from her parents.

But in Montreat Ruth would face the heartache of long separations from the man she loved. In the evenings, as the sun sank behind the wooded mountains of North Carolina, she would head to bed, to read, pray and sleep with Bill's tweed jacket tucked under her arm for company.

But not all of Billy's meetings were held far away. He did his best to get back to Montreat in between his journeys, but on occasion he spoke at meetings closer to home. One of those meetings was held at the Ben Lippen Bible Conference in the North Carolina Mountains. Billy was addressing a youth night, only there was a problem. The song leader was absent and there was no one to take his place. Then from somewhere a young, athletic, Californian named Cliff Barrows appeared. Cliff was twenty-one years old and on his honeymoon. Billy was told he could sing and had some musical ability. Smiling broadly at the new recruit, Billy exclaimed, 'Well, there's no time to be choosy!' and with that Cliff Barrows and his wife were on the team.

Billy had no need to be dubious about Cliff's musical talents. As soon as he got on the stage with his pretty young wife at the piano it was obvious that the fellow had ability. His face beamed, his eyes twinkled and his presence on the stage was warm and engaging. Then there was his fine baritone voice and excellent trombone playing!

That night saw the beginning of a long partnership in preaching and song between Billy and Cliff, one that would take them across the country and across the world.

***

One of Billy Graham's first international visits had been to the United Kingdom, when it was still recovering from the ravages of World War II. At that time Youth for Christ was booked to do a whirlwind tour of England, Scotland, Ireland and Wales. Billy had for the first time come face to face with the deprivation suffered by the general population of the country due to rationing. Rationing meant that every morning for his breakfast all he had to eat was a tomato stuffed with bread. As there was little heating to speak of, Billy went to bed fully clothed in order to keep warm.

On his return to the U.S. Billy never forgot the courageous and faithful people he had met in that war-wearied country. He had a burning desire to return to preach the gospel. And return he would, several times over the coming years.

'It was so dark and grimy,' he commented to a friend one evening. 'On nights like this you couldn't really go outside at night. The blackouts still continued. Everything was pitch-black, and the winter of 1946 was the coldest winter in a hundred years. With fuel shortages you can imagine what a difficult time the people were having. But despite all that they smiled and their courage and faith taught me a lesson that I will never forget. It wasn't long before we headed back. This time I managed to persuade Ruth to come with me.'

'How did she feel about that?'

'It was difficult. She had to leave Gigi behind. But the baby was fine living with her grandparents in Montreat. Cliff and his wife Billie came with us which got a bit confusing with names. That's why Cliff has always called me Bill, in order to distinguish between me and his wife.[1] But in the end Ruth couldn't stand being away from our baby girl. Two months into the campaign we agreed that she should return home while I continued to preach in Europe.'

'That must have been hard for you too?'

Billy nodded. 'The separations are always hard. We knew they would come and we know there will be more of them. But Ruth has made it very easy for me. She supports me in so many practical ways and in prayer. She is a very spiritual person. In fact, one of her recent letters told me that wherever I am she will go with me in her mind and pray for me constantly.'

The problems and difficulties that faced the Grahams could have broken other marriages but in God's strength this couple stayed strong and together.

As Billy Graham returned from the European campaign he brought with him a new vision.

'We can run one-day rallies like we've always done, but why not run meetings for a week, maybe even two! We should be praying about this.'

---

[1] Cliff Barrows is the other person, in addition to Billy's wife Ruth to call Billy Graham, Bill.

So plans were made for Billy Graham's first mass evangelism meetings. This was to be a three-week long campaign held in Los Angeles in September 1949. However, before that could take place Billy had several key issues that he had to work out with the Lord.

In Modesto, California, Cliff Barrow's childhood home, Billy and the team came to a monumental decision. They designed what would later be called the Modesto Manifesto. Billy was conscious of how other evangelists had failed and was adamant that he would be different. He did not want their work for the Lord to be soiled by scandal and disgrace. So Billy called the team together to talk this issue over.

'I want us all to go to our rooms for an hour or so and list all the problems that you can think of that may face evangelists and evangelism.'

The men returned with remarkably similar lists. And with that they made a set of resolutions that they vowed to keep. These rules would guide them throughout their future evangelistic work.

1. There was always to be accountability as far as finance was concerned. The team would do all they could to avoid financial abuses. They wouldn't make such a big thing of the offering and instead would depend as much as possible on any money raised by the local committees.

2. They vowed never to be alone with another woman other than their wives. In this way they

avoided temptation and any appearance of evil that might be commented on by the press and therefore disgrace the cause of Christ.

3. They promised never to criticise local churches or pastors. They would cooperate with all who would cooperate with them.

4. Finally they vowed never to make false or misleading publicity regarding the attendance or conversion figures. They would leave it up to the local authorities to judge how many people attended.

These were points that the young men would follow for the rest of their lives. These decisions focused their hearts and minds on the mission they were called to by God. They were determined to make these vows central to their lives and ministry.

Another crucial issue for Billy was a personal one. At a conference in Forest Home, California he witnessed the blessings of someone totally committed to the Word of God and the confusion caused by someone who questioned the truth of Scripture.

The conference was run by Miss Henrietta Mears, the Director of Education at First Presbyterian Church of Hollywood and a female mentor for Billy. 'Her enthusiasm for the Lord Jesus Christ is so contagious... and the faith that she has in the integrity of the scriptures!' Henrietta's stand stood in stark contrast to others who attended the conference like Chuck Templeton. He was one of a group of young theologians who were expressing their doubts about the authority of the Bible.

'Can we trust this book completely?'

'How can we know if it's true?'

'Maybe parts of it are true, not all of it?'

Billy Graham was troubled and began to study his Bible with even greater intensity.

'Paul says that "All Scripture is given by inspiration of God."' Billy told himself one evening. 'Jesus says that "Heaven and earth shall pass away but my word shall not pass away." If Jesus never gave any indication that the Scriptures were false then surely I can believe in them too?'

Billy knew that he had to get this settled there and then or he wouldn't be able to continue doing what he was doing. As he walked in the moonlight he fell to his knees in prayer. Holding his Bible open he said, 'Lord there are many things in this Book that I do not understand. But God, I am going to accept this Book as your Word by faith. I'm going to allow my faith to go beyond my intellect and believe that this is Your Inspired Word.'

From that moment on Billy Graham never doubted God's Word. He quoted the Bible and firmly believed that he was quoting the very Word of God – with power. Then came Los Angeles.

Puff Graham!

Ruth knew the importance of Los Angeles for her husband and his ministry. 'It's the largest city in America next to New York and Chicago and they're going to put up the biggest tent in the history of evangelism.' Ruth's parents smiled. The meetings had been scheduled to run for three weeks, but now amidst all the press coverage and media exposure it was rumoured that the three weeks would be extended. Ruth described the banner on display outside the tent, 'It's huge. Bill's picture is on it and a list of all the others assisting on the platform, like Cliff Barrows and Beverly Shea. Underneath Billy's name they've printed the words, "Dynamic Preaching, Glorious Music and 6,000 Free Seats."'

'Six-thousand?' Ruth's mother gasped.

'Yes!' her daughter exclaimed. 'But they're getting more than 6,000 coming and they're turning even more away. The tent can't hold all the people who want to hear the gospel.'

'Praise God!' Mrs Bell exclaimed.

Ruth nodded her head slowly. 'It's all down to God,' she declared. 'The credit belongs solely to him. It's the secret of everything that's been happening down there. God's been answering our prayers.'

'You'll be heading out west again, won't you?' Ruth's mother enquired a day or two later. 'Billy will need you with him.'

'Yes, I'll have to go,' Ruth acknowledged. 'But I just can't be there all the time, or go with him to all his preaching events. I know that it's good to be there, even just to hold his hand on occasion, but I've got the family to think of. I knew the separations would be hard. I even knew they'd be long and often. In fact, I frequently think about how my life before Billy was my training ground for him,' she confessed.

'What do you mean?' her mother asked, but with a knowing look in her eye.

'You know…' Ruth sighed. 'All those separations we had in China. The fact that I had to be packed off to Korea to go to boarding school and then sent across the Pacific to go to college.'

'Hmm,' her mother murmured. 'I particularly remember how reluctant our young spinster was to go.'

Ruth smiled. 'That's true. I had my life all planned out, but God's plans were different.'

'And better,' her mother stated.

'Yes, better,' Ruth agreed. 'For a start I've been allowed to be part of Bill's life, supporting him in his work, supporting the Lord as he works through my husband… and what a work! Why, you know they've decided to extend the meetings to four weeks in Los Angeles,' Ruth commented.

'I had heard you mention that they were considering it. I didn't realise it had been decided though.'

'No. Well they had wanted to be sure it was the right thing and then something happened that convinced them.'

'What exactly?' Mrs Bell asked.

'Well, there's a country and western singer, Stuart Hamblen. You might not have heard of him but he's got a radio programme, what you might call a children's Cowboy Church on the air waves.'

Mrs Bell looked puzzled. 'So he's a Christian?'

'Ah,' Ruth paused before starting again. 'Let me start at the beginning. He's the son of a Methodist minister and was certainly brought up in a Christian home in Texas. But as he says himself he 'left it all behind.' He lived a double life and didn't mind broadcasting gospel songs on the radio as long as he could carry on drinking and gambling. However, Suzy, his wife, has been praying for him for sixteen years and finally she persuaded him to come to Bill's meetings in Los Angeles. During the second week though, Bill began to get under Stuart's skin. The guy began to get really annoyed with the preaching, with the singing, with everything ... but especially with Bill. When Bill would preach he'd say, 'That fellow's lying.' When they gathered the collection he'd tell his wife, 'This is a racket!' Even the singing wasn't good enough. But when Bill began to speak about how there was someone in the tent that night who was a phoney – that was it. Stuart Hamblen rose up from his seat and actually shook his fist in Bill's face. Then he stormed out of the tent.'

Mrs Bell gasped at such behaviour. Ruth continued with her tale, 'Stuart immediately headed out on a drinking spree, going from bar to bar, but nothing seemed to work. The only thing left for him to do was to head home. As soon as he got in the house he woke his wife up with a yell, 'Let's pray!' But even that couldn't calm his soul. It was 2.a.m when Stuart decided that since Bill was the guy who had started all his problems he could be the one to sort them all out. So he phoned him up there and then and Bill agreed to meet with him at the hotel.

But it wasn't a simple matter of Stuart turning up at Bill's hotel room, saying a simple prayer and then going home again – everything sorted and happy. No sir. Bill doesn't agree with that kind of easy salvation which is no salvation at all. This had to be the real thing.

It took several hours before Stuart finally gave in and relinquished every area of his life to the Lord's control. The very next morning Hamblen got on to his radio station and told his audience that that evening he was going to go down to the front at Billy Graham's evangelistic meeting, that he'd given his life to Christ.'

'Praise the Lord!' Mrs Graham said again.

Ruth nodded her head, 'It's caused quite a sensation I can tell you. Yet it was the sign the team were waiting for and the meetings have been extended.'

***

The next time campaign meetings had to be extended was a good example of how God is in control of every part of human life, even the media. All of a sudden there was even more media interest than usual. Billy Graham turned up at the meeting one night and instead of the small selection of local reporters there were journalists and photographers everywhere. It was a bit confusing at first, until someone came up to Billy and explained, 'You've been kissed by William Randolph Hearst.' In the reporter's hand was a piece of paper that looked as though it had been torn off a wire transfer machine. On it were just two words, 'Puff Graham'.

What on earth did that mean? And who was William Randolph Hearst? And why was he kissing people?

Well William Hearst was a millionaire. He owned twenty-eight newspapers and eighteen magazines. Even from his sick bed William Hearst was in charge of a very lucrative media empire. He had umpteen editors just waiting to get instructions from him. His word was law.

So, being kissed by William Randolph Hearst, meant that you were going to be given a lot of really good media attention. And that was what happened to Billy Graham.

How did this all happen? What made William Randolph Hearst decide to make Billy a national celebrity? Well, among his large staff William Hearst had a middle-aged maid named Hedla who always listened to *Songs in the Night*. When Billy Graham was in Los Angeles she went along to several of his meetings and then one morning, while she was helping to make Mr Hearst's bed, he questioned her about the young preacher.

'What's your opinion of him?'

The maid gave such a glowing and enthusiastic account of the meetings and of Billy Graham himself that Hearst was soon giving his editors explicit instructions to 'Puff Graham!' This was a Hearst expression his editorial staff understood very well. Billy Graham was to get the maximum publicity. So twenty-eight newspapers and eighteen magazines were told to 'talk up' the young evangelist, give him more column space and better editorials.

As a result Hearst's editors and reporters flocked to the evangelistic meetings and as soon as they started doing that all the other newspapers jumped on the bandwagon. Soon Billy's name was known right across America, and articles were appearing in major magazines such as *Time* and *Life*.

As everyone wanted to find out who this Billy Graham was and what he had to say for himself, even more people began to flock to the meetings in Los Angeles. Criminals and con men, actors and sports personalities, people from all walks of life decided to go and hear Billy, but they were really going to hear the good news of Jesus Christ. It wasn't the messenger that was important but who that message was about – Jesus Christ.

Many who came because of their curiosity left the meetings with their lives changed and their hearts turned towards the living, loving Saviour. Sins forgiven, eternal life and the blood of Christ shed for sinners were Billy's subjects. He didn't change the Word of God or preach a different gospel to make it easier for the Los Angeles' crowd to stomach. The man who was in the middle of this media frenzy and public interest was still the same Billy who had knelt before the Lord accepting the authority of scripture. He was still the same young man who had preached in Baptist churches across North Carolina. He'd come a long way since the days when he'd practised on squirrels and rabbits, but his gospel was the same because it was the same good news of Jesus Christ and the cross that had saved Billy at his first evangelistic meeting all those years ago in Charlotte.

***

When Ruth went west to visit her husband during the last couple of weeks of the evangelistic campaign she found him furiously studying the Word, desperate to find material for more sermons. Time and time again he was being brought back to the Bible, back to simple gospel preaching, biblical preaching and a truthful humility.

Billy Graham wrote at that time, 'I want no credit or glory. I want Jesus to have it all!'

It was Jesus who deserved the glory! It was because of God that there were the New Year meetings in Boston in 1950. Sixteen thousand people squeezed into Boston Garden, the city's largest indoor arena. More than 1,000 people spontaneously got up out of their seats to come forward and ask Jesus Christ into their lives.

Then there was Columbia, South Carolina, twenty New-England towns from Rhode Island to Maine, back to Boston and then on to Ocean City, New Jersey, where he met the President of the National Religious Broadcasters and another chapter of his life began.

After some very persistent pressure from various people connected with broadcasting, such as Dr Theodore Elsner, Walter Bennett and Fred Dienert, Billy Graham came back to public broadcasting as a method of evangelism. It didn't happen overnight, however, as Billy had to be persuaded first of all – and that wasn't easy. Walter Bennett and Fred Dienert actually caused Billy quite a bit of stress as they kept pushing and pushing for a national weekly broadcast. They just wouldn't give up. Billy rejected the idea as being far too much work and a distraction. Time and time again he sent those two men away, ignoring their pleas and telling them straight that the $92,000 required to start up a prime-time radio slot of this nature was just out of the question.

Walter and Fred weren't about to give in gracefully. When Billy heard that they were hanging around in the lobby of his hotel he resorted to using the fire escape to avoid them. But despite his reluctance to face up to these two gentlemen Billy was gradually brought round to the idea of getting on the radio once more. The only problem was that he couldn't see a way around the financial hurdles. The sort of money they required wasn't just lying around for the taking. Amazing things had to happen before that sort of cash materialised. When Walter and Fred were finally given their interview with him, Billy Graham learned that the two broadcast enthusiasts had secured a $2,000 donation. However, they needed a lot more than that to start a radio broadcast. So Billy did what he often did in situations like these. He got on his knees and prayed.

'Dear Lord, you know that I believe we should do this. You know that I don't have any money. Lord you know I don't know where the money is and that I'd go out and get it if I had the time. So it's up to you, if you want this, you'll have to prove it to me by giving me $25,000 by midnight.' This was a tall order. It was a huge sum of money in those days.

However, that night Billy was up again on the podium preaching to a congregation of about 20,000 people. When it came for the time of offering he didn't mention a word about the radio programme. The collection that was being gathered was for the expenses of the evangelistic meetings and nothing else. Only after the offering had been taken did Billy speak of the radio broadcast. Instead of going straight to some mega-business who would have supplied the cash at the flick of a switch or the slip of a pen, Billy had decided to come to God and to those who had come to listen to God's Word. He spoke about the radio station idea in a simple matter-of-fact way. There was no emotional pressure laid on. Billy knew that if God wanted it, then God would do it.

'If any of you folks would like to be part of all this, I'll be in the office back there at the close of the service tonight.'

After the address was over, and the final prayer offered to God, people got up to leave the building. It took a long time for them to filter through, but when the bulk of the people had exited the tent a long line began to form at the office. An old shoe box was found and soon it was filling up with pledges and gifts, $1,000 here, $200 there – coins and cents, a widow's $5 bill. The final figure was just below their target but it was an amazing collection all the same.

'Hey Billy,' someone yelled. 'You've collected $23,500. It's a miracle.'

But Billy wasn't so quick to judge. He'd asked for $25,000 before midnight and he wasn't going to start a radio station for anything less. Some of the team felt terribly disappointed. However, when the dejected team arrived back at the Hotel three envelopes were waiting to be presented to Billy. One envelope was from a person who just hadn't had the time to wait in line that evening. Each envelope enclosed a pledge, one for $1000 and the other two for $250 each. The total now stood at $25,000!

However, that sudden influx of cash caused a small problem. Where did you keep that sort of money? Initially it stayed in someone's sock drawer overnight but the following morning it would have to find a bank account. If it went into Billy or Cliff's bank account they'd be charged income tax on it. A quick telephone call was all that was needed and plans were soon put in place for the Billy Graham Evangelistic Association. It had been something that had been planned for some time. It had certainly been in people's minds when the Modesto Manifesto was written. Now the plans moved up a gear and became reality. Ruth, Billy and two others were the founders of the Association, and it was Ruth who decided on the name for the new radio broadcast.

'What's the whole emphasis of what you do Billy?' she asked him. Not waiting for an answer she replied to her own question, 'It's that people should make a decision for Christ.'

So *The Hour of Decision* was born, first broadcast on November 5th 1950, it still goes strong today.

And it was from there on that the early team of evangelists began to learn on their feet what it really meant to head up a major Christian organisation. In 1951 a man called Dawson Trotman came on board. He was the founder and leader of another Christian ministry organisation called *The Navigators* but his input was invaluable to the future campaigns.

A feature of a Billy Graham evangelistic meeting, even today, is what goes on after the altar call. Follow up - where every enquirer would be counselled - became a huge and important aspect to the ministry. Enquirers were also corresponded with after the event.

Until Dawson Trotman came on board Billy and the platform team had been exhausting themselves with the preaching and worship as well as being involved in counselling afterwards. Dawson Trotman taught Billy a valuable lesson which was summed up in the question he asked him one day, 'Don't you believe that God has given us gifts too?'

From that moment on Billy concentrated on the preaching, and the counselling team was allowed to use their God-given abilities to answer the questions of the thousands of people who came to the front to ask for prayer.

Other men like Willis Haymaker were influential in encouraging Billy Graham and the team to work closely with the churches in whatever area they worked in. With the influence of men like Haymaker and Dawson Trotman the Billy Graham meetings soon became well organised and excellently prepared. As always, the focus was on reaching people with the good news that salvation is offered free to all who will believe in Jesus Christ, and turn to him for forgiveness of their sins.

However, with the newness of it all, and so many things for the new association to learn, there were bound to be teething troubles. One was a photograph that appeared in a newspaper after meetings in Atlanta.

'He can't stand it!' one of the team exclaimed to a colleague as they held up *The Constitution* newspaper, glaring at the two pictures that had offended Billy Graham so intensely. 'That picture of Billy waving goodbye to the crowd outside the baseball park, and the other photo of the collection that the ushers gathered up, they imply that evangelism is just a racket – a scam to fleece people of their money.'

'Yes,' agreed his colleague. 'There are a lot of people who think that.'

And it was this false impression that Billy wanted to stifle once and for all, at least with the BGEA.

Advice was sought and soon a decision was reached.

'There's one way that will work,' a respected minister concluded. 'And that is for Mr Graham to be paid a regular salary just like any other minister. It would be paid to him by the Association, and it would be about the same amount as a minister from any typical large church.'

Billy nodded in agreement. It made sense and it would finally see the end of the 'love offering' that they had to gather at each event in order to cover the living expenses of the team members. From that moment on Billy and others in the Association could finally offer their services for free. Any money went straight to the Association and, no matter what cash was raised, the individual evangelists received their salaries and nothing more. It was all above board and there was no room for any criticism or cheeky newspaper photographs either.

In the midst of all this expansion and excitement it could easily have been forgotten that Billy Graham had a young wife and a growing family back home in North Carolina. The Grahams did at least have their own house now, literally just a stone's throw away from Ruth's parents. But the beginnings of the new association had major implications for the young family. Billy's responsibilities meant a lot more than just a massive pile of mail to respond to. Eventually it meant that the whole family became a bit of a tourist attraction. Ruth would often discover 'friendly intruders' making their way down the drive to 'visit' with the Grahams. Once she was quite alarmed to see a strange pair of eyes peeking at her through her bedroom window. The kids, who by 1952 consisted of three girls, Gigi, Anne and Ruth, and one boy, Franklin, had their own way of dealing with intruders. They would charge money to those people who asked them to pose for photographs – just a little extra pocket money! However Ruth had had enough of it. In her opinion it was time that people realised that the Graham family members were not public property.

As Billy's meetings and campaigns became more frequent and further afield, the young family grew accustomed to their father's goodbyes. The same scene occurred countless times on the doorway of the Graham household: a neatly dressed mother, anxiously clasping the hand of a puzzled little girl with blonde pigtails, waving a farewell as a tall man in a blazer and hat lifted some large, heavy suitcases into the trunk of the family car. Yet Billy and Ruth made sure that the whole process was as painless as possible for the young Grahams. Many times, however, Billy's eyes filled with tears as soon as his head was turned and his children were out of sight. Even though he knew that this was something that he had to do, it was hard to leave behind the wife and family he loved so much.

The separations were difficult for everyone, including Ruth. Seeking solace in her Bible and her journal she often prayed and wrote poetry in order to get through the heartache.

A Brush with History

Ruth's heartache had to be shielded from her young family. Both she and Billy made sure that family farewells weren't tearful, emotional events. The couple would say goodbye to each other in private and then the children would wave goodbye to Daddy at the doorway. These separations could be hard, but over the years Ruth came to the knowledge that their children were her work, her mission field.

She often tried to be with her husband for at least some of every major campaign but this wasn't always possible. Her calling was to run the family home and one of Ruth's responsibilities was to arrange the purchase and building of a new house.

In the year 1954 a good deal was offered them on some land not far from Montreat, but far enough away from the main roads to discourage those pesky sightseers. The land was good value at about $12.50 to $14 an acre.

Privacy continued to be a problem, particularly as Billy Graham became a well-known name across America. Ruth and Bill insisted on keeping their family out of the spotlight and away from media interest. They would not allow them to be displayed at the campaign meetings. With their own land purchased, and the threat of persistent tourists investigating the Graham family home, now was the time to start planning the move.

The plans for the house were soon up and running – one thing Ruth really wanted in them was lots of fireplaces – but it was to be a while before the plans became an actual family home. In the meantime both Ruth and Billy agreed to take part in one of the Association's first overseas campaigns based in the United Kingdom. The evangelistic meetings made Billy Graham a household name in the U.K., and Christianity a nationwide topic of conversation but sadly the British press were not so welcoming.

Billy had experienced the positive spin that the media could put on a campaign. He had, after all, found out what it was like to be 'kissed' by William Hearst. However, the beginning of his campaign in the United Kingdom was very different. Headings were splashed across front pages and editorials, 'Now this Yank says we're heathens!' and 'Silly Billy.'

Criticisms came right, left and centre. Billy arrived in the U.K. to a very antagonistic media. It wasn't long since the end of the Second World War and, although it was getting back on its feet the United Kingdom was still in one news reporter's words 'battered and squeezed as no victorious nation had been before, disillusioned almost beyond belief.'

The BGEA had planned a three-month slot of evangelistic meetings. It wasn't going to be easy, however, because the British press were out to cause trouble. Billy really needed Ruth's support during this time and she was only too glad to give it. However although she agreed to accompany Billy this time there wasn't a single day when Ruth wouldn't have cheerfully packed her bags and headed back across the Atlantic to Gigi, Anne, Ruth and Franklin.

On Billy's arrival in the U.K. one of the team heard a newspaper columnist comment on his mode of transport. 'When Jesus was on earth, he rode a lowly donkey. I cannot imagine Jesus arriving in England on a great ocean liner!'

Billy's colleague fired back, 'Listen man, if you can find me a donkey that can swim the Atlantic, I'll buy it on the spot!'

Billy seemed to be able to respond to any question or criticism in a gentle, unruffled manner. He was obviously being given help from God. He didn't rise to the bait and yell back at the reporters or criticise them. He met with them and answered any question that they wanted to ask. He even agreed to meet one particular reporter at his local pub for a drink. Billy didn't drink alcohol, but enjoyed the lively conversation and a lemonade. Eventually the tide began to turn. Reporters began to acknowledge the fact that Billy Graham was a skilful communicator as well as a really patient guy.

So London was made ready for what would be a series of meetings lasting from March through to

May of 1955. Harringay Arena had been booked with some trepidation. The arena had never, in its long history, been filled to capacity by any speaker for even one night, far less several. The first meeting was scheduled to start at 7 p.m. The weather that day was foul. It rained constantly, and by the time the evening arrived the rain had turned to sleet. Billy and Ruth were just getting into their car to be driven to the arena when they received a message.

'We've only got about 2,000 people sitting in their seats and the meeting starts in half an hour.' Ruth gasped, 'The arena seats 12,000!'

Billy nodded grimly. Three hundred press and photographers were waiting at Harringay. It was just the kind of headline the British press were looking for. 'Harringay Washout.' 'No show for Billy Graham.'

'The press are apparently taking photographs of all the empty seats,' Billy sighed. He could just imagine the photographers snapping away gleefully. They had been proved right.

As Billy and Ruth were driven slowly through the streets of London towards Harringay they held hands tightly, not uttering a word. All they could do was trust in God. He would help them to face whatever was around the corner.

When they arrived at Harringay the sight before them brought tears to their eyes. In the half hour that Billy and Ruth were en route to the arena thousands of people had flooded out from the Underground to fill the empty seats. In fact many people who had travelled all the way across London to attend the meeting found on arrival that they could not get in. The building was full for the first time in its existence. And as the final notes of the hymn 'Blessed Assurance, Jesus is Mine' echoed around the arena Billy Graham stepped up to the microphone to do the task which God had called him to do all those years before – preach! Billy preached on John 3:16, 'For God so loved the world, that the gave his only begotten Son, that whosoever believeth in him should not perish but have everlasting life.'

And with that simple message Billy explained to the rapt congregation that 'No sin has ever escaped the eyes of God, but no sinner has ever escaped his love. There is only one way back to God and that is through Jesus Christ.'

Over the following days and weeks people began to realise that to get into the Harringay meetings you had to be there on time. The arena would be jammed full at least an hour before Billy was due to get up on the podium. Police estimated that during the first week alone at least 30,000 people had failed to get in. Future meetings at the Harringay Arena were linked by landline relays to 405 different churches throughout the country. It became a prominent feature of the London campaign. This meant that people outside the arena could listen to the gospel message being preached.

Other venues were soon sought out. Trafalgar Square was packed with people; it was like the Victory celebrations all over again. At Hyde Park the police estimated that there was a crowd of over 50,000 to listen to Billy preaching on, 'God forbid that I should glory, save in the cross of our Lord Jesus Christ.'

And that text seemed to sum up the country at that time. Christians, who had been too tongue-tied and awkward about sharing their faith, became quite open and matter-of-fact about Christianity. Billy Graham had all of a sudden made it easy to talk about religion, be it in the cafeteria, pub or over the dinner table.

The meetings seemed to be changing the city of London itself. People sang hymns on the tube, men and women smiled at each other as they travelled, there was an atmosphere of joy about the place. The number coming forward at the end of the meetings was totally unexpected. It was more, far more, than had ever come forward at any of the American campaigns. Social climbers with cut glass accents sought salvation along with washer-women and pick-pockets with cockney twangs. In fact one pick-pocket had to turn to the man in front of him as he made his way down to the front of one meeting and say, 'I'm going to have to return your wallet now.'

And so it went on… night after night… month after month and then May arrived. There were two further meetings to be held on the final day of the London event, and they were scheduled to take place in the Wembley and White City Stadia, the two largest stadia in the capital. On that day Billy Graham preached to about two hundred thousand people, at that point the largest religious gathering in British history.

Once again he preached a simple gospel sermon, concluding with the words, 'You can go back to the shop, the office, the factory, with a greater joy and peace that you have ever known. But before that can happen you must commit yourselves to Jesus Christ. You must make your personal decision for him. And you can do that now. Choose this day whom ye will serve.'

And with that men, women, teenagers, families began to get out of their seats as thousands had done before them in Harringay and Atlanta and New York and Charlotte – to come down to the front, to pray, to ask the Lord Jesus Christ to forgive their sins and to take control of their lives from that day forward.

The London meetings were not the end of Billy Graham's work in the U.K. On May 25th, he and Ruth were scheduled to leave for Scotland for a brief holiday before travelling to Scandinavia, Holland, West Germany and France.

On the morning that they were due to depart the telephone rang. A few minutes later Billy came through to Ruth and exclaimed, 'I don't believe it.

I've just turned down the Prime Minister, I've turned down Winston Churchill!'

'What? You've done what?' she gasped.

'He wanted to meet me at 10 Downing Street tomorrow, but I explained we're scheduled to get on a train today. I told his secretary that I felt honoured but that it just wouldn't be possible for me.' Billy looked at Ruth's incredulous face and sighed. 'I know, dear, I've turned down a meeting with Winston Churchill. I probably won't get another chance like that again.'

Minutes later the phone rang for a second time and Winston Churchill's secretary spoke once more. 'Would you be able, Mr Graham, to meet with the Prime Minister at noon today?' the polite English accent enquired. 'He has an appointment scheduled for twelve-thirty with the Duke of Windsor, who is flying in especially from Paris, but he could see you just before that. There is a slot available - a few minutes.'

Billy didn't need to think twice, and with hardly any time to feel nerves or anxiety he was soon standing before one of the most famous doors in the world. As he entered No. 10 he was given strict reminders of his time limit. He was only allowed twenty minutes as the Prime Minister was on a tight schedule that day. Billy entered the Cabinet Room and was soon, on his own, alongside Winston Churchill. The typical cigar was propped in the Prime

Minister's mouth, and a selection of daily newspapers were spread around him on the table. Mr Churchill rose to shake his hand and Billy towered above him. Churchill was a lot shorter than Billy had imagined him to be.

'I want to congratulate you for these huge crowds you've been drawing,' said Mr Churchill.

'That's God's doing, believe me,' Billy replied.

'That may be,' he replied, peering at this rather interesting American. 'But if I brought Marilyn Monroe over here and she and I went together to Wembley, we couldn't fill it.'

That light-hearted remark was the beginning of a meeting that would last considerably longer than the scheduled twenty minutes. Billy Graham, mindful of the fact that he was not only speaking to an individual, but to one of the most influential men of the twentieth century, was careful how the conversation went. He'd had experiences in the past with powerful men of state where he had made blunders and had caused offence simply because of his over enthusiasm. However, this time would be different. Winston Churchill asked questions, Billy Graham answered them. 'What is it in your opinion that has filled Harringay night after night?'

'It's the gospel of Christ,' was Billy Graham's direct answer.

The conversation covered topics such as world politics, the church, morality, hope. In fact, Winston

Churchill shared with Billy his own despondent lack of hope for the world, 'I have no hope. I see no hope for the world,' Winston Churchill exclaimed, as he pointed to the headlines on the daily newspapers. 'Murders. War. Communists. That's all the papers print these days,' he sighed. 'I am a man without hope. Do you have any real hope?' he asked.

Billy Graham listened to that and in seconds made the decision that this wasn't just a general comment about the world wide political situation, this was a personal plea for help from one man to another. Billy responded to that question with another, 'Do you have hope for your own salvation?'

Winston Churchill looked him in the face and said, 'Frankly, I think about that a great deal.'

So taking out his New Testament Billy explained the way of salvation to Winston Churchill.

After making the Duke of Windsor wait another fifteen minutes for his lunch meeting, Churchill agreed to Billy's request that he be allowed to pray with the Prime Minister. Churchill actually thanked Billy for suggesting it. After the prayer, in which Billy had asked the Lord to help the Prime Minister with what was a difficult and stressful job, and thanked the Lord for being the one true hope for the world and for individuals, the two men shook hands and Billy was shown to the door. Winston Churchill's last words to him were, 'Our conversation shall remain private at least as long as I am alive.'

To this Billy Graham agreed wholeheartedly. And Winston Churchill's conversation with him remained unreported during that famous man's lifetime.

The Graham's got on the train the next morning feeling that they had brushed against history.

A Different Europe

It was without doubt a different Europe that Billy Graham was visiting, far different from the one that had signed the Armistice just days before his birth. It was different too from the Europe that had so recently clambered out of another World War as the continent had been carved up between the allies, but they weren't really allies any more. Winston Churchill and his counterparts talked of 'The Cold War', 'The Communist Threat' and nowhere better summed this up than the city of Berlin.

The Berlin Wall[1] had not yet been built so when Billy Graham arrived to conduct evangelistic meetings in the city thousands arrived to hear him from the Eastern Zone where the Communist regime was in charge.

It must have been a stressful time preparing Billy for the meetings and helping him to recover from chronic kidney pain. One hundred thousand people were expected to attend the meeting to be held in the place which was commonly referred to as 'Hitler's

---

[1] The construction of the Berlin Wall began in 1961 and it closed the border between East and West Berlin for twenty-eight years. East Berlin was under Communist control whereas West Berlin was governed by the Western, democratic powers. The Berlin Wall was demolished in 1989.

Stadium.' It had been built by the Nazi Dictator during his chancellorship and was notorious as the venue for the German Olympic Games, the one where Jessie Owens, a black American, had virtually snatched the gold medal from Hitler's prized Aryan athletes. Hitler had, in fact, stormed out of the stadium in a giant huff when the medal was awarded to the American. Yes, Europe had certainly changed now that Adolf Hitler had gone.

Many in Billy Graham's team must have commented on the amazing fact that God had arranged for a young man from a dairy farm in North Carolina to come and preach a message of hope in such a place as this. It was the very place where the Swastika had been raised high. The words 'I am the way, the truth and the life,' were the only flag Billy was flying that day.

As he approached the podium, preparing to speak to the near-capacity crowd, there was a steady rain falling. It kept some people away, but it didn't stop the preacher. He was ready for this – despite exhaustion, despite more negative press coverage, despite the kidney stones. He was ready because he was leaning on God for strength and trusting in the message that God had given him. That message was the message of Christ and the cross.

A friend had once said to him, 'How can anyone be converted without having at least one single view of the cross where the Lord died for us? Preach about the cross, Billy. You must preach about the blood that was shed for sinners there. That is where the power is – when we talk or preach about the cross.'

Several days after the final Berlin meeting Billy and Ruth Graham were sailing back across the Atlantic towards an enthusiastic homecoming welcome. What cheered Billy more was the radio phone message that came from the organisers of the Berlin event.

'Listen to this, Ruth,' Billy gasped, as he rushed into their cabin. 'Sixteen thousand Germans have filled out decision cards. The follow-up programme is swamped. They're organising meetings in churches across the city to cope with the demand.'

'Wonderful,' Ruth exclaimed. Her eyes lit up with enthusiasm. 'What a wonderful time it has been. God has blessed us, hasn't he?'

Billy nodded his head and smiled. 'Now it's home, sweet home,' he declared. Neither could hide the longing to see their children once again.

Less than a year later Billy Graham was heading back across the Atlantic for the Scotland meetings that were to last for six weeks. These meetings would bring about key changes for the Billy Graham Evangelistic Association. The first of these was that Billy was coming to the country with the full support of all the major denominations in that country. That had never happened before. Because of this amazing goodwill the BGEA decided to do things a little differently this time. Up to that point the evangelistic team had always invited ministers and church leaders to send people to the counselling classes. Now they would invite the ministers to try out the classes first.

'You see, the ministers were a bit nervous about what Billy was going to be teaching,' one of the evangelistic team said with a mischievous smile, while Billy was still in the room. 'They wanted to make sure he was genuine, that he wasn't going to be teaching heresy to their congregations.'

Somebody laughed at that before asking just as mischievously, 'So how did it go? Did the clergy disagree with your theology? Did the Scottish ministers send you packing?'

'No, Sir!' was the exclamation. 'They're behind us all the way!'

'We put their minds at rest,' Billy joined in. 'They did the counselling classes first. As soon as they understood what it was we were going to be teaching they got behind the whole campaign. They understand what we're about now. That's why they say they're going to go back to their congregations to drum up support. They're going to ask the church-goers to attend classes. I can't wait to see how many people will come.'

How many people did attend? Thousands! The number of people who applied for the counselling course broke new records.

'I can't believe it! Praise God! The highest numbers we ever had at counselling classes before this was Harringay with 2,500. We've never had anywhere near that number in the states! Here in Scotland we've got 4,000 people taking our classes!'

From then on the Billy Graham Evangelistic Association always explained the ethos of the campaign and the follow-up methods to the clergy first.

The counselling classes during the All-Scotland Campaign proved an encouragement in other ways too. They actually became one of the key methods that God would use to bring people to himself. People who were sent to the classes by their churches in order to bring other people to Jesus Christ, were actually brought to Christ themselves. Up to that point they had had no real knowledge of what it meant to be a Christian. They hadn't had real faith. They hadn't been born again. They hadn't realised what it was to be in a personal relationship with Jesus Christ. When they were taught this simple message in order to teach it to others, God's Holy Spirit taught it to their own hearts and they believed and were saved.

Billy arrived in the U.K. on board a French liner, *The Liberté,* that had sailed out of New York Harbour to arrive in Plymouth to hymn-singing and a warm greeting from fellow Christians. This was something that would be repeated throughout his journey to the land of his ancestors. The train journey was on the overnight sleeper and at the first Scottish village where the train stopped Billy was caught off-guard by a crowd of well wishers. Still in his pyjamas he had to hastily throw on an overcoat in order to greet another hymn-singing welcome party. At every stop along the line more welcome committees emerged to greet Billy. This was such a relief to the preacher as he had been anxious and worried about the campaign. The warm welcome was just what he needed.

Billy Graham then entered the city of Glasgow ready to preach. The city itself had an inspiring motto that would have encouraged any preacher. It was, 'Let Glasgow flourish by the Preaching of the Word and the Praising of His name.' These words declared a past that had at one point been focused on God and his Word – perhaps it would be again?

'Just one point, Mr Graham,' a minister, who was attending one of the planning meetings, spoke up. 'I think it might be best if we didn't have any altar call. The people here are just not used to it. There's no tradition of an altar call in any of the major denominations of this country. And besides, the Scottish people are far too reserved for that.'

However, Billy believed that the altar call was necessary. On the first night the Kelvin Hall was filled to capacity. Billy Graham finished preaching and then asked those who wanted to make a decision for Jesus to come to the front of the hall. Nobody moved.

'They were right,' Billy thought in himself. 'Nobody is coming.' It was crushing. He had felt especially close to the congregation that night and yet it looked as though nobody had been challenged or affected by the message at all.

Returning to his seat Billy sat down and bowed his head. Doubts and fears attacked him. Just then Billy realised that all over the country, even across the world people were praying for him, for the meetings, for the people who would listen and respond to the Word of God. God would hear and answer these prayers. Billy knew it and joined in. As he finished his prayer he glanced up and in those moments of brief prayer the scene in the Kelvin Hall had totally changed. People were getting out of their seats and streaming down the aisles from every part of the auditorium. Many who made their way to the front that night had tears in their eyes. Ministers and church leaders who sat on the podium with Billy Graham openly wept with joy at the sight of so many people seeking what their souls so urgently needed. The nation had a spiritual hunger, and the Lord Jesus Christ had been brought to them to satisfy that hunger.

On Good Friday a sermon preached by Billy Graham on the central message of the cross of Christ was broadcast across the nation. The viewing figures for this programme were second only to the numbers that had viewed the coronation two years earlier. But on this occasion the Queen and Prince Philip were watching the television too. A few days later an invitation arrived from Windsor Castle inviting Billy to preach at the Royal Chapel after the U.K. campaigns were complete.

During the final two weeks of the Glasgow campaign Ruth arrived as planned to join him with their nine-year-old daughter, Gigi. Billy's letters to Ruth during his time away were proof of how much he had missed her and how much he needed her by his side.

'You have no idea how lonesome it is without you.'

'You are the only one who ever really understands...'

'You have no idea how often I have listened to your advice.'

'I'll be counting the days till you arrive.'

So it was that Ruth was there with her husband as he preached at Windsor Castle to the Queen and the Royal family and she joined Billy with the Queen for lunch afterwards.

What was the legacy for the nation of Scotland? The campaign had drawn 2.6 million people with over 52,000 making decisions for Christ. An 18,000 seat stadium had been filled night after night for six weeks. Many day-time meetings had also been held. Thirty-seven relay centres had been set up throughout the whole of Scotland bringing the message to the rural and outlying areas. Ibrox Stadium itself saw a crowd of 50,000 come to hear the gospel being preached.

An astonishing 100,000 attended the Hampden Park meeting. Then there was the national broadcast that reached 30 million people. By the year 1959, the Glasgow Bible Institute reported a marked increase in applicants. Across the nation there was an increase in the number of men applying for the ministry as well as candidates for missionary service.

***

The following year Billy Graham began a campaign of meetings in India, his first major campaign outside the West. He was overjoyed to be visiting this country and bringing the message of salvation to its people. India was a country of magnificent extremes - incredible beauty that took your breath away and gut-renching poverty that made you weep. Billy Graham had always been fascinated by India and now he was finally going there. He would witness at first hand the sights and sounds of the East, so very different to the sights and sounds of North Carolina or any other place he had ever visited before.

These differences meant that Billy had a problem. 'How do I communicate the good news of Jesus Christ to these people?' he asked himself. 'Most of them have no concept of the Bible. Their culture and thinking is so different from the West.'

Billy and others in the team prayed continuously about this problem. It was not going to be easy, but shortly before their arrival in India Billy got his answer. Their plane flew over Mount Sinai where God had given the Ten Commandments to Moses. In the distance they could see the land of Israel where Jesus had lived and worked and preached. Somewhere in that country was a little town called Bethlehem where he had been born in a stable and laid in a manger.

Where the great continents of Asia, Africa and Europe intersect a baby had been born, the Son of God, and this child had become a man and had been punished for the sin of his people on the cross. Those people came from every tribe and tongue and nation across the world. That was the answer to Billy Graham's dilemma.

'I am not here to tell you about an American or a European,' he would say. 'I am here to tell you about a man who was born in Asia. He had skin that was darker than mine, and he came to show us that God loves all people. He loves the people of India and he loves you.'

Those who heard him began to realise that Christianity wasn't just for Europeans, Jesus Christ wasn't just for people who had white faces. Christ had come for all.

And this was the message that was preached in India's major cities such as Bombay, Madras, New Delhi and Calcutta.

At every meeting in India Billy Graham preached on the same verse of scripture, John 3:16: 'For God so loved the world that he gave his only begotten Son that whosoever believeth in him should not perish but have everlasting life.'

There were riots and disturbances outside some meetings, particularly in Bombay, but in Madras Billy still preached to a crowd of 40,000. Over the three days he was there 100,000 people heard the gospel and 4,000 made a decision for Christ. Twelve thousand copies of the Gospel of John were distributed among the attentive crowds. And in the rural area of Kottayam instead of a stadium the congregation were seated in a amphitheatre cut out of the side of a hill by the local women. Seventy five thousand people came to hear the preaching, many of them bringing palm leaves with them to sit on.

The land of India left a definite impression on Billy: the culture, the people, the poverty, as well as the desperate need of Christ. He had his eyes opened to so many new experiences yet he realised that human beings are the same the world over and that the gospel of Jesus Christ, when preached in simplicity and power, can change the heart of any man, woman or child no matter what their religion or skin colour. In later years, when asked what country he would like to go back to, Billy Graham would always say, 'India.'

It had been a hectic and busy time for Billy Graham, full of so many landmarks and new experiences: prime ministers, queens, heads of state, flights, liners, crossing the Atlantic, crossing continents, and now it was time to go home. But this time it was a return to the home that he and Ruth had dreamed about and planned. A tourist-free home; a home in the mountains; a family home; a home of their very own.

105 Degrees in the Shade

It was a lovely home to come home to. Ruth made
it that way. She had made a house that fitted into
the landscape of that remote mountain side. The
mountain side was too far away for garbage collection
and too far away for curious tourists to come driving
round – paying the kids to pose for photographs and
sticking their noses up to the window panes for a
closer look! However, just in case, the Graham kids
had their own way of making sure that no trespassers
intruded on the family home. They made a large
sign for the end of the driveway which warned any
uninvited guests that the Graham family also might
include a dog or two. The sign read, in no uncertain
terms, 'Trespassers will be eaten!'

Ruth had bought old timbers and bricks to give
their new home that authentic mountain look. It was
the perfect place for Billy to return to and recharge,
to be a daddy once more to his kids and a husband
to his much-loved wife. Her letters during his times
away from his family were his life-line and support.
Now back with his wife, children, cat, dogs and even
three pet sheep, Billy could relax. But there was
more to focus on than family fun. A new study built
in a part of the house away from the children's noisy

play meant that Billy had time to study and prepare himself spiritually for the next lot of meetings. A big campaign planned for New York caused Billy to come to God in prayer, time and time again. On top of the mountain behind their home Billy would stand for hours seeking God and asking in faith that he would touch the city of New York and prepare its people for the gospel of Jesus Christ.

The New York campaign raised many problems before it had even started and Billy was on the phone as often as three or four times a day to the organisers. Every time it seemed that a new, unsolvable problem had arisen, and then the situation would be resolved… again! But the more he thought about it, the more Billy worried. The more he studied, the more inadequate he felt.

'I'm not ready for this,' he'd say, as he bowed his head in despair within the confines of his study. 'This is one of the biggest cities in America and everybody says that it's going to be difficult. But I don't believe God wants us just to go and preach in easy places. Over half the people in New York don't go to church. Every nationality in the world lives and works within its streets. There are more Italians there than live in Rome and more Irish people there than live in Dublin. You'll find more German people living in New York than live in the city of Berlin. They say that whatever happens in New York happens throughout the world. If New York can be reached for Christ the effects will reach out to the world. Whatever happens I do believe that God will receive the glory and the honour from this campaign.'

With tears in his eyes and a prayer in his heart Billy Graham knelt again before his Lord and his God. This city was a heavy burden on the evangelist's heart and one that would send him to his Saviour in prayer again and again and again.

The team was certainly ready and prepared to do their best along with 40,000 bumper stickers, 25,000 songbooks, 100,000 copies of the Gospel of John, 35,000 posters and 650 billboards posted at key locations throughout the city. Madison Square Gardens was the venue, and once again record-breaking numbers of people came to hear the gospel being preached.

'All your life you've been searching for peace,' Billy declared from the platform. 'You've been searching for peace, joy, happiness and forgiveness. I want to tell you before you leave Madison Square Gardens this night, you can find everything that you have been searching for in Christ. He can bring that inward deepest peace to your soul. He can forgive every sin you've ever committed. And he can give you the assurance that you are ready to meet your God, if you will surrender your will and your heart to him.'

The campaign lasted for sixteen weeks in total and during that time more than 2.3 million people heard the Word of God being preached. Many thousands made professions that they had made a decision for Christ. Some of these professions came by mail from those who had listened on radio or watched on television. Throughout the campaign bookstores reported an increased demand for Bibles. The press reported on the campaign in general, and on Billy in particular, in a favourable manner. Even the cartoonists gave him good press. Billy Graham knew the importance of press coverage and never missed the opportunity for an interview or a television broadcast. When asked to go on the Steve Allen show he had the opportunity to give his testimony to 40 million Americans on the NBC Television network, an opportunity that he didn't need to think twice about.

But towards the end of the campaign the venue was changed. The Yankee Stadium was booked and many people said that it couldn't be filled. However, on the hottest day of the year, (105 degrees in the shade) the stadium was filled to overflowing with attendance reaching more than 100,000 inside and an overflow of thousands outside the gates. An aerial photograph showed the park teaming with people: all seats filled, people standing in every available spot they could find. Billy Graham knew that this was God at work. And when there was no room available to ask people to come forward at the altar call Billy requested that people just stand where they were if they wanted to make a decision for Christ. There was no way to count the thousands that rose from their seats to show the world that – yes – they believed in Jesus Christ as their Saviour.

Many people came to Madison Square Gardens, The Yankee Stadium, even the meeting held in Times Square. Two notable people who attended the meetings at that time were Vice President Richard Nixon and Dr Martin Luther King. Dr King gave the opening prayer at one of the meetings. This was in fact typical of Billy Graham and his ministry. From the very beginnings of his campaign meetings, even those held in the Deep South where segregation was still the norm, Billy refused to separate the whites from the blacks. Although he was not the national voice against segregation that Martin Luther King was, he was the nation's preacher and his stand against segregation was through the Word and through his practical witness. Billy Graham always refused to segregate his congregation. 'There is no segregation at the foot of the cross,' was his declaration if ever questioned on the subject. So from the early days it had been known that a Billy Graham meeting was unsegregated. Whites and blacks and coloureds sat together to hear the gospel.

The New York meetings were, in fact, the first where it was realised that the BGEA needed to focus more on getting the African American population to attend the meetings. How were they to do this?

Thankfully, Billy Graham had employed an African American on the BGEA team. Billy asked him for his advice which was, 'Go to where these people are. That's the way to bring them in.' So Billy made it a priority during the campaign to visit the black churches and community centres, meeting with people and just showing them that these meetings weren't just for white folks, that God looks on the heart not on the outside appearance.

As well as doing this, the BGEA began to reach out to the large Hispanic population in America. For the first time Billy Graham was translated into a different language while in his own country. A Spanish-speaking meeting was held during the day at Madison Square Gardens.

It was almost as though every meeting he preached at and every campaign the association was involved in, something new began. There were always new records being broken. Time and time again God proved the doubters wrong as capacity crowds filled stadia that nobody thought could be filled. But Billy was always careful about making too much of the numbers. It was easy to get roped into focusing on the thousands when the real story was about individuals. Yes, thousands and hundreds of thousands and millions did hear the gospel, many of those did come to Christ, the meetings did fill stadia to capacity, all that was true. There were great choirs, huge attendances and many people being counselled, but what was needed was lives changed, hearts changed, people changed. Billy freely admitted when the campaign was over, that it didn't really seem as if the city of New York was all that different. 'But lives have been changed,' he exclaimed 'and that's what matters.'

He was right. Many lives were changed: politicians and diplomats, wealthy business men and actresses, were just a few of those who came to Christ during the New York Campaign. However, out of the thousands, many more who made a decision for Christ came from ordinary, hard-working families.

One story in particular stands out.

In the counselling room after an evening meeting there was a woman standing near the front with tears running down her face.

She was just an ordinary mother, wearing her workaday clothes. She wasn't anything special in the world's eyes, but Jesus had saved her and she was so grateful. However, her counsellor could sense that there was something wrong, something was bothering her. Between her tears and her sobs she explained, 'My son is a heavy drinker and I'm afraid that he will beat me up if he ever finds out that I've become a Christian.'

The counsellor opened her mouth to speak. But, before she could utter a word, another voice spoke out from the back of the room.

'It's OK Mom, I'm here too.'

An exhausted Billy Graham knew that through stories of lives changed that the campaigns, like the New York one, were definitely worth it. However, they were draining. He lost at least twenty pounds in weight during the sixteen weeks preaching and they never ran a campaign of that length ever again. But they did go back to New York and they did carry on the campaigns all around the world, starting next with Australia.

This time Ruth was not able to come. A fifth child had been born to the Graham family, a little boy called Ned. Ruth had her responsibilities at home and could not leave even for a short while. But this was going to be no flying visit. Billy Graham would be away from home for five or even six months. It would be a strain for all concerned. Cliff Barrows also had to face the same wrench from his family.

One new thing happened on the Australian campaign. It was the first time that follow-up material was designed for use with children. It had been the local committee's idea, and the BGEA decided to go along with it. However, it was such a good idea that Billy and the team decided to have children's follow-up material available for every campaign after that.

The local Melbourne committee were also absolutely certain they would have massive crowds. Billy and the others hoped they were right but they weren't convinced at first. When the rented stadium was filled to overflowing, and Billy had to preach two sermons each night, the team realised that the local committee had been right. They even had to find a bigger venue. The attendance reached 70,000.

The final service was scheduled for the Melbourne Cricket Ground, a huge facility that had been expanded to a capacity of 105,000. A crowd of 50,000 was expected. But when every seat was filled the cricket ground authorities had to lock the gates. Word was sent to the directors of the meeting that there were still thousands outside desperate to get in. The final crowd estimate was 143,750, a new record for the stadium and for Billy Graham himself. It was the largest audience that he had ever addressed up to that point.

Further trips were scheduled to Tasmania and New Zealand, Sydney, Perth, Adelaide and Brisbane. Sydney broke Billy Graham's record once more with an estimated 150,000 crowd. By the end of their final meeting in Australia well over three million people had attended the meetings in person and 150,000 people enquired about how to become followers of Christ. But once again the story was not about the numbers but the changed lives. A safe-cracker heard the gospel and gave his life to Christ. Later he and his counsellor met up with his gang to tell them what had happened. Between them they explained the gospel and why the one-time thief would no longer be helping them in their burglaries.

Then there was the divorced man who came to the meeting with his girlfriend only to see the woman who had been his wife walk forward to the front to give her life to Christ. Convicted of his sin, he realised that he needed to be reconciled to God and to his wife. So he got up out of his seat and went to stand beside her at the front. In addition to them others came forward too, including a man who had embezzled a large sum of money from the bank where he worked. He confessed to his crime the next morning and, so impressed his boss with his decision, that instead of being sacked and prosecuted he was kept on staff. The boss went to the meetings the next day and gave his own life to Christ.

What had Billy Graham to say about all this?

'For what has happened in Australia I want to give the glory and praise to God. I hope you will soon forget about us except to pray for us. I'm here to represent Jesus Christ, the King of kings and the Lord of lords; to Him be the glory and the praise and the honour.'

And what else can be said? Throughout the sixties and seventies Billy Graham and his team went back and fore across Africa, back to Asia, South America, throughout several cities in North America, even back to Europe and Australia. But in all those countries he never once openly criticised a political regime from the pulpit. He made his stand in other ways. For instance, he had always refused to visit South Africa because of their policy of racial segregation entitled Apartheid. For as long as that ideology remained unthreatened within that nation Billy Graham would not hold an evangelistic service there. It was his opinion that if we cannot meet at the cross of Christ as brothers then we cannot make it at all.

Billy Graham eventually did preach in South Africa to mixed-race crowds when the first stranglehold of that regime began to give way. And that wasn't the only political regime to come to an end during his life time. Communism also crumbled.

However the 1960s were a troubled time in America as well. The Western nations were up to their necks in a nuclear arms race. America was struggling with race riots. Martin Luther King was shot. There was the Vietnam war. There were protests against the war. There was a presidential assassination... a president that Billy Graham had met in person.

In fact, throughout his ministry, Billy Graham met several presidents. His first experience of the White House was in his early days as a young evangelist. And that experience taught him a crucial lesson about politics.

His first meeting with President Truman showed him the necessity for confidentiality. He had naively reported his interview with Truman word for word to the press waiting on the White House Lawn. This was a mistake that he never committed again.

Over the years Billy met and advised many, if not all, of the U.S. Presidents such as John F. Kennedy and Richard Nixon. Lyndon B Johnson, Nixon's predecessor, was perhaps one of the Presidents with whom Billy had the best and most relaxed relationship. And it was the message that he gave at Johnson's funeral in 1973 that was carried into Communist Europe.

'For the believer the brutal fact of death has been conquered by the historical resurrection of Jesus Christ. For the person who has turned from sin and has received Christ as Lord and Saviour, death is not the end. For the believer there is hope beyond the grave. There is a future life! The Bible says in John 11:25-26, "I am the resurrection, and the life: he that believeth in me, though he were dead, yet shall he live: And whosoever liveth and believeth in me shall never die."

And when that message was finally brought into the Eastern block, where Communism had held sway ever since the end of the second world war, it found a ready audience... an answer to prayer that Billy had prayed as far back as 1959.

Moscow Tourist

In the year 1959 Billy Graham had been involved in several campaigns. There was one country he visited however as a tourist: The Soviet Union. He went there specifically to pray. In the large stadium in Moscow he sat down and looked out across the vast array of seats.

'Lord God,' he prayed fervently. 'May I live to preach here one day to people filling these seats, hungry for your Word.'

But before The Soviet Union would hear Billy Graham preach on its soil other European countries issued him with invitations to speak within their churches and stadia.

It wasn't easy negotiating an entrance visa to a Communist country, particularly if you were a visiting Christian evangelist! Communist countries, by their very nature, were atheist and anti-Christian. Many were actively persecuting Christ's followers behind their borders and a considerable number of Christian believers were actually imprisoned for their faith.

Hungary was the first Communist country to invite Billy Graham to preach. Soon afterwards other Eastern-bloc countries did the same.

East Germany's invitation meant that Billy Graham could visit Wittenberg where he was allowed to preach in the pulpit of Martin Luther, the great German Reformer. In honour of the occasion he chose Luther's favourite verse of Scripture, 'The just shall live by faith,' Romans 1:17.

'Just as spiritual renewal came five hundred years ago in Martin Luther's day and changed the course of history, I pray that today spiritual renewal might once again sweep the German Democratic Republic and the world.'

In the early 1980s an invitation finally arrived from the Soviet Union asking Billy to speak and preach in that country. But this also involved attending an international conference on the perils of nuclear war. Billy didn't know if he should go or not and he sought advice from U.S. Presidents past and present.

President Regan, who was in the White House at that time, believed that, even though the conference was a notorious venue for Communist propaganda, Billy Graham should go. 'I believe that God works in mysterious ways,' he said. 'I'll be praying for you.'

So Billy went and delivered his message at the peace conference. During his seven day visit he was also allowed to preach in the Moscow Baptist Church as well as the Russian Orthodox Cathedral of the Epiphany. Human rights were never far from his mind, particularly as he met with the Siberian

Seven, religious refugees who had been living in the basement of the U.S. Embassy for four years. Billy also had a list of 150 believers who were thought to be prisoners of conscience at that time. This he presented to a member of the government while telling him that many Christians in America felt that their fellow believers in the Soviet Union were being oppressed, and that while this was going on the chances for better relations between the two countries were very slim.

However, there was some doubt back in the U.S. as to whether Billy Graham should actually be doing this kind of international travelling.

'Are you aware,' a young reporter asked, 'that the Soviet government has used you for their propaganda?'

'Yes, I am aware of this,' Billy replied. 'But I have been using them for my propaganda, and my propaganda is more powerful. We are using them to preach the gospel of Jesus Christ to their people.'

The 1982 trip to Moscow was soon followed up by a 1984 trip to Leningrad, Tallinn, Novosibirsk and Moscow. When asked by a government official if he loved Communists Billy fervently replied, 'Yes, every one of them, and Jesus Christ also loves them.'

Throughout the Soviet countries Billy Graham's message was that Communism would not win and neither would Capitalism, – but that ultimately it would be the Kingdom of God that would be the victor. This message was listened to avidly throughout the Soviet countries. Every meeting and gathering had dozens of tape recorders recording Billy's every word. These tapes would be passed round and listened to again and again.

Although Billy Graham's meetings were tolerated by the Communist powers they often found the large turnouts embarrassing. To reach the thousands waiting outside the churches loudspeakers were slung up on to trees and nearby apartments. The Secret Police in Romania had not given permission for speakers to be put up and demanded that they be taken down. The man who put them up insisted that he wouldn't remove them. 'Look at all these people,' he exclaimed. 'They'll kill me if I take the speakers down. You take them down.' The policemen looked at the crowds who were glaring back, and decided to leave the speakers up.

Then towards the end of the 1980s, things really began to change. A stadium in Hungary seated 75,000, but a total of 110,000 turned up to hear the gospel being preached. Every seat was filled and every spot of grass was used for seating. Hungarian radio broadcast the services live. Months later, by the end of December 1989, the change that many had been waiting and praying for finally arrived. The Communist party was dissolved in Hungary, Poland, East Germany, Czechoslovakia and Romania. The forty year reign of a godless atheist political regime was finally over. In 1991 the Soviet Union itself came to an end. Billy Graham could see God's pen as if it were writing history. The Bible was having an impact in the modern day world. Hearts and minds of people across countries and national boundaries were being changed for ever.

Finally, in 1992, Billy saw the answer to his own personal prayer of 1959. Instead of only being allowed to preach inside Russian churches, the Moscow Olympic Stadium was made available and was filled to capacity. Fifty thousand people squeezed into the 35,000 seat auditorium. His vision of being able to preach to a capacity crowd in Moscow was fulfilled. God had answered his prayer and many people rejoiced at that.

Where politicians and the media had doubted, Billy Graham had believed. The president at that time, George Bush, said, 'It takes a man of God to sense the early movement of the hand of God.' Eastern Europe and Russia had been made ready for the gospel and now they were drinking it in. They were hungry for it. Many were open to God.

It can be easy to forget, however, that Communism was not just a European problem. China, Ruth's childhood homeland was also Communist. Ruth had always dreamed about taking Billy there to see the place where she had been brought up. The love of that country and its people had never left her. During the time of political upheaval in Eastern Europe, Billy and

Ruth were also invited to the People's Republic of China. Billy preached in three large churches there and also in one of the unofficial house churches.

However, it was revisiting her childhood home and greeting old childhood friends, that gave Ruth most joy. Her family now grown up she was delighted to be able to take Billy to where she had spent almost seventeen years of her life. Young Franklin went too and they visited little villages and farmhouses, saw water buffalo and peasants, sights which she remembered so clearly from long years ago.

The crumbling of European Communism didn't mean that international confrontation was a thing of the past. There were still countries and states that were closed to the gospel. There were national leaders who were openly antagonistic to freedom – religious and otherwise. As a new millennium loomed the old problems of sin and man's inhumanity to man were just as prevalent as ever. The world changed, but humanity did not. International politics was turned on its head but the message of Christ remained unaltered. The words that flew high above countless Billy Graham Evangelistic meetings remained the same, 'I am the way the truth and the life.' It was still the gospel that was central to the Billy Graham campaigns.

Global Relief

One of the things that Billy Graham was accused of early on in his preaching career was that he focused too much on the gospel and not enough on social issues. Now that criticism was unfair as you cannot really separate the two. The gospel is a message of hope, of spiritual hope, but it is also immensely practical in its message. Billy Graham knew that. He knew that you didn't go out to the world with words and no action. That was why global relief effort became such a central part of the BGEA's work. This part of their ministry meant that the Association was there at the times of tragedy in America and across the world. Wherever U.S. troops were stationed, Billy would try to visit them in order to take them a message of peace, the peace of Christ that is beyond all understanding.

In Korea in 1952, and Vietnam in 1966 and 1968, Billy Graham preached in the middle of war zones. He preached about the love of Christ as he visited the wounded; the sound of army helicopters in the background ferrying in more dying men from the battlefield.

Warn-torn countries like Lebanon and Northern Ireland were visited in order to bring comfort and a message of hope. Where natural disasters had taken the lives and livelihoods of many the BGEA would often be there with practical support. And then when the horror of terrorism began to stalk the land of America, at the worst times of tragedy, Billy and Ruth Graham would join the nation in mourning for the lost.

Many people trembled at the bombing in 1995 in Oklahoma City unaware of what the new millennium would bring in its wake. But as people questioned why God allowed such things to happen, Billy was there with counsel. He never claimed to have all the answers. At the memorial service that Billy attended for the victims of the Oklahoma bombings, he went straight to the heart of the matter.

'How can things like this happen? Why does God allow this to take place? First, it is a mystery. I have been asked on hundreds of occasions why God allows tragedy and suffering. I have to confess that I can never fully answer that question. I have to accept, by faith, that God is a God of love and mercy and compassion even in the midst of suffering. But the Bible tells us that Satan is real, and that "He was a murderer from the beginning". And it also tells us that evil is real, and the human heart is capable of almost limitless evil when it is cut off from God and his moral law. Times like this will do one of two things: they will either make us hard and bitter and angry at God, or they will make us tender and open. I pray that you will not let bitterness poison your soul, but that you would turn in faith and trust to God, even if we cannot understand. My prayer for you today is that you will feel the loving arms of God wrapped around you, and you will know in your heart that he will never forsake you as you trust him.'

Almost the exact same message would be needed again six years later.

***

In the twentieth-century people often asked one of two questions: 'Do you remember where you were when Neil Armstrong first set foot on the moon?' or 'Do you remember what you were doing when you heard that President Kennedy had been assassinated?'

However, the beginning of the twenty-first century started with an incident of its own that those of us living in its aftermath think of as one of the days that we will always remember. It was a day that will go down in history, an infamous day, a terrifying one.

At some point in the future you may very well ask the following question: 'Can you remember what you were doing on September the 11th 2001?'

It was a day that changed the world.

On the morning of September 11, 2001, nineteen al-Qaeda terrorists, Islamic extremists, hijacked four commercial passenger jet airliners. The hijackers crashed two of the airliners into the World Trade

Center in New York City, one plane into each tower, resulting in the collapse of both buildings soon afterwards. A third airliner was crashed into the Pentagon in Arlington County, Virginia, while the passengers and members of the flight crew on the fourth aircraft attempted to retake control of their plane from the hijackers. That plane crashed into a field near the town of Shanksville in rural Somerset County, Pennsylvania. In addition to the nineteen hijackers, 2,973 people died; another twenty-four were reported missing and presumed dead.

New York and Washington were both targeted. Many lives were lost. If the planes hadn't crashed, and the Trade Center hadn't collapsed, these people would have gone about their days working in offices, or getting on and off planes for business meetings or holidays. The emergency services wouldn't have been called out to the flaming towers. They wouldn't have been crushed by falling masonry when the buildings finally collapsed. But the attacks did happen and many lives were lost or changed forever.

Heroic stories of courage and tragic tales of loss have been told about the men and women who suffered on that day. There was so much heart-ache, so many people mourning, so many people with a question to ask. And the question they asked was 'Why?'

Once again Billy Graham was called upon to give an address on a national day of mourning, to comfort the nation, to respond to their grief. This message was the same message that had been given six years before. It was the same message that had comforted the thousands in Eastern Europe during the last days of Communism, it was the same message that had given hope to the millions who had suffered under Nazi Germany. It was the same message of hope that people had been calling out for since the First World War, since before Billy Graham was born, since the very first human beings committed the very first sin.

Billy Graham was the same preacher who had stood up in Harringay and Madison Square Gardens. He preached the same message he had preached in Trafalgar Square and in Oklahoma. But it was a much older man that made his way up the steps to the pulpit on the morning of September 14th 2001.

Presidents past and present were there to listen to what he had to say, but there were also mourning relatives, friends and colleagues; People who were weeping and angry and full of questions and fears sat before him.

Billy had preached across the world in war-torn lands, but never before had a battle of this ferocity come to his home country. For an American, a tragedy of this magnitude on U.S. soil was unimaginable. It was the stuff of Hollywood – unbelievable. But it had happened. As Billy Graham made his way to the book board to lean on it and look out at the searching, seeking congregation, to preach again to a nation and the world, he spoke once more about hope, salvation and truth.

'We come together today to affirm our conviction that God cares for us, whatever our ethnic, religious or political background may be.

'The Bible says that He is "the God of all comfort, who comforts us in all our troubles."

'No matter how hard we try words simply cannot express the horror, the shock, and the revulsion we all feel over what took place in this nation on Tuesday morning. September 11 will go down in our history as a day to remember....

'But today we especially come together in this service to confess our need of God. We've always needed God from the very beginning of this nation, but today we need Him especially. We're facing a new kind of enemy. We're involved in a new kind of warfare and we need the help of the Spirit of God. The Bible's words are our hope: "God is our refuge and strength, an ever present help in trouble. Therefore we will not fear, though the earth give way and the mountains fall into the heart of the sea..." (Psalm 46:1,2, NIV).

'... It may be difficult for us to see right now - this event can give a message of hope - hope for the present, and hope for the future.

'Yes, there is hope. There is hope for the present

because I believe the stage has already been set for a new spirit in our nation.

'One of the things we desperately need is a spiritual renewal in this country. We need a spiritual revival in America. And God has told us in His Word, time after time, that we are to repent of our sins and we're to turn to Him and He will bless us in a new way.

'There is also hope for the future because of God's promises. As a Christian, I have hope not just for this life, but for heaven and the life to come … We never know when we too will be called into eternity. I doubt if even one of those people who got on those planes, or walked into the World Trade Center or the Pentagon last Tuesday morning thought it would be the last day of their lives. It didn't occur to them. And that's why each of us needs to face our own spiritual need and commit ourselves to God and His will now.

'Here in this majestic National Cathedral we see all around us the symbols of the cross … the cross tells us that God understands our sin and our suffering, for He took them upon Himself in the person of Jesus … And from the cross, God declares, "I love you. I know the heartaches and the sorrows and the pains that you feel. But I love you."

'The story does not end with the cross, for Easter points us beyond the tragedy of the cross to the empty tomb that tells us that there is hope for eternal life, for

Christ has conquered evil and death. Yes, there is hope ... "Fear not, I am with thee; O be not dismayed, For I am thy God, and will give thee aid; I'll strengthen thee, help thee, and cause thee to stand, upheld by my righteous, omnipotent hand."

'My prayer today is that we will feel the loving arms of God wrapped around us, and will know in our hearts that He will never forsake us as we trust in Him.'

***

Eventually the sounds of falling debris and search parties fell silent at Ground Zero[1]. The tragedy had set country against country and people at each other's throats. A new kind of war had arrived - Terrorism. Every day there seems to be a new victor but there is always a vanquished, a victim, a tragic consequence of evil. There are now countless graves that scream at the world that there never has been a war to end all wars. Treaties have been signed and will be broken. There will be wars and rumours of wars. But the message of hope will be proclaimed ... a message as old as time itself... the message of a Saviour ....The message of Jesus Christ.

---

[1] Ground Zero - This is the name given to the area that once contained the Twin Towers and surrounding buildings. It is a phrase that is often used to describe an area that has undergone violent activity and where emergency vehicles congregate to give help and aid.

So in the slightly edited words of an unnamed college student from last century: 'At each critical epoch of the church, God has a chosen instrument to shine forth his light in the darkness. Men like Luther, John and Charles Wesley, Moody, Billy Graham and others who were ordinary men, but men who heard the voice of God ... It has been said that Luther revolutionized the world. It has been said that Billy Graham changed lives and changed continents. It was not him, but Christ working through him. The time is ripe for another Luther, Wesley, Moody, Graham. There is room for another name in this list.'

Who will that be in this century? Will it be you?

Thinking Further
Chapter 1
What did girls find attractive about Billy? What is attractive in you? What does the Bible say about appearances? Read 1 Samuel 16:7.

What did Billy do to the school bus? Have you ever done something like that? Have you hurt others? How did you feel? Billy wasn't interested in the Bible or his spiritual life. What is your reaction to spiritual things?

Chapter 2
Going to church was not an option for the Graham family. Do you go to church regularly, sometimes or not at all? How important is church attendance?

Do you think Billy's upbringing made a difference to how he related to others? Has your upbringing made a difference in your life?

Why is it important to read the Bible and pray every day? Read Acts 17:11, Colossians 4:2.

Chapter 3
Mordecai Ham, the evangelist, traveled around telling people how to get their sins forgiven. Have you ever heard an evangelist preach?

At the meetings Billy tried to hide from the evangelist, but God still spoke to him. Billy was convicted of his sin. Have you ever felt sorry for the sin in your life?

Billy didn't give his life to Christ immediately. Sometimes we try to put things right ourselves, when all Jesus wants is for us to come to Him. Read Matthew 11:28-30, 1 Peter 5:7.

Chapter 4

When Billy first preached he didn't feel that he would be any good. However, God can use weak person to do great things for Him. Do you believe God can use you?

Billy wanted to give himself completely to Christ and to see his country called back to God. If you had a similar burden what should you do?

When Billy was in love he prayed about the situation. Why should you ask for God's help in seeking a marriage partner? Read 2 Corinthians 6:14.

Chapter 5

Why did Billy preach the Gospel whenever he could? Do you share your faith with others? Read Luke 24:46-48.

Billy felt there was something missing when he preached. What difference did prayer make? What influence did Ruth Bell have on Billy's life? Where did Ruth's heart lie? Have you ever been torn in two directions regarding a decision you had to make?

Chapter 6

Billy and his wife were separated a lot due to his preaching engagements, but in God's strength the difficulties they faced only strengthened their union together. Do you find separations difficult?

How can we know that the Bible is true? Read 2 Timothy 3:16.

Billy's evangelistic team listed the problems they might face. Apart from those mentioned, can you think of any other problems that might arise?

Chapter 7

What influence did Billy have on Stuart Hamblen, the country and western singer? Have you ever had a similar influence on anyone? What does the saying, "Puff Graham" mean? How did the money for the radio programme come in? Can you think of times when your prayers were answered. Did you thank God for his help? Read Psalm 37:4.

Chapter 8

In 1955 the first UK campaign got under way. How many people arrived on the first night? What was it that drew them? Read John 6:44; John 12:32.

Which scripture verse did Billy preach on that night? What is your favourite scripture verse? Which Prime Minister did Billy meet and share the way of salvation with? Have you shared your faith with anyone?

Chapter 9

A friend said to Billy that he should preach about the blood that was shed for sinners. How important is the blood of Christ? Read Hebrews 9:22.

Why did a minister say there shouldn't be an 'altar call' in Glasgow? If you were at one of Billy Graham's meetings, would you go forward?

The Kelvin Hall, Glasgow, was filled to capacity, but no one went forward at the 'altar call' at first. What changed the whole atmosphere?

Chapter 10

Billy did not segregate his congregation. Whites, blacks and coloured people sat together. Read Romans 10:12-13, Galatians 3:28.

Billy learned the importance of confidentiality when speaking with people. Do you gossip? What was the message Billy carried into Communist Europe? What are your thoughts about death, heaven and hell?

Chapter 11

Who was Martin Luther and what was his favourite verse of scripture? Name the communist countries where Billy was asked to preach. Where are we called to preach? Read Matthew 28: 19-20.

What was one of the teachings of communism? Would you find it hard to live in such a society?

Chapter 12

Global relief effort became a central part of the BGEA's work. The association was there at great times of tragedy. How important are social issues to you? What was Billy's answer to tragedy and suffering? How do you react when things go wrong in your life? Do you believe that God understands?

Billy's address after the September 11th tragedy in 2001was one of hope. What is our hope? Read Colossians 1:27.

Just Get Up
Out Of Your Seat

From Richard Bewes

Billy Graham is the most effective world evangelist we have had since the New Testament Apostles. For some individuals it takes a virtual lifetime to achieve prominence on the world's stage – but in the case of Billy Graham, it all began to happen at an incredibly early stage.

Imagine me as an excited teenager, singing with thousands of others on the London underground, as we made our way to Harringay Arena to hear Billy Graham. Picture me if you can at the close of this sensational three-month long campaign, sitting up high in the stands, joining 120,000 others at Wembley Stadium.

Little did I think that thirty-five years later Billy would be speaking again in that historic stadium – but this time with me to chair his meeting! Such has been the time-span embraced by this remarkable ministry. A few years later would see me joining Noel Tredinnick and a sixty-piece orchestra in Moscow. God had answered Billy's prayer of many years earlier, during Communist rule, that one day he would be given the opportunity to preach in that great Olympic Stadium.

Thank you Catherine for the careful research and animated writing put into this so-inspiring story of our time.

RICHARD BEWES O.B.E.
West London

How to become a Christian

The Bible says, "For God so loved the world that He gave His only begotten Son, that whoever believes in Him should not perish but have everlasting life" (John 3:16).

In Romans 3:23 we read that all have sinned. Sin separates us from God. You can be as sincere, moral and as religious as possible but this won't bring you back to God. God is the only one who can save you from your sin.

The Bible says, "He personally carried the load of our sins in His own body when He died on the cross" (1 Peter 2:24 TLB).

The Bible also tells us "Whoever calls upon the name of the Lord shall be saved" (Romans 10:13).

Without Christ - you will be separated from God but by believing in Christ you will not suffer eternal death. This is because the gift of God is eternal life through Jesus Christ His Son.

There are four things you need to do to receive Jesus Christ as your Saviour:

1. **Admit** you have a spiritual need. "I am a sinner."
2. **Believe** that Jesus Christ died for you on the cross to take your sin upon Himself and to provide forgiveness, or full pardon, for you.
3. **Receive**. Pray for Jesus Christ to enter your heart and life.
4. **Repent**. This means, with God's help, to be willing to turn away from your sins.

Now that you're a Christian

When you follow Jesus Christ this means that God has forgiven you. New believers need to get their Christian lives off to a good start so here are four simple tips for a healthy spiritual life.

The Bible: Everything we need to know about God and how to please him can be found in the Bible. Spending just fifteen to twenty minutes a day reading God's word will be of huge benefit to you throughout your life.

Pray: Praying to God is important. It doesn't matter where, when or why you pray. Pray to God every day. Confess your sin, praise him, tell him you love him, thank him and bring your requests to him. He is listening.

Go to Church: New Christians need to meet with other believers at a local church. The church is a place where you will be taught and spiritually nurtured. They will help you to grow in your faith.

Share Your Faith: Jesus commands Christians to share their faith with others! When you talk about what Jesus has done in your life this will encourage you and others.

How to become a Christian and *Now that you're a Christian* were inspired by material produced by the Billy Graham Evangelistic Association. To read advice on the Christian life and becoming a Christian go to the Billy Graham Evangelistic Association website: www.billygraham.org

Billy Graham Time Line

1918   Born William Franklin Graham, Junior.
       World War I ended.
1934   Billy became a Christian.
1939   World War Two began.
1939   Ordained to the ministry by a Southern
       Baptist Church.
1943   Earned bachelor's degree, Wheaton College,
       Illinois. Marries Ruth McCue Bell.
1945   Birth of first child, Virginia.
       World War II ended.
1948   Birth of second child, Anne.
1949   Los Angeles campaign which lasted six weeks.
1950   Billy Graham Evangelistic Association
       founded.
       'The Hour of Decision' weekly radio
       programme began.
       Birth of third child, Ruth.
       Evangelistic meetings in Boston Garden.
1952   Billy wrote his first book, *Peace with God*.
       The twelve week Greater London campaign.
       Birth of fourth child, William Franklin III.
1955   Six week campaign in Kelvin Hall, Glasgow.
1957   Billy holds meetings in New York.
       Television career began.
1958   Birth of fifth child, Nelson Edman.
1961   Berlin Wall was built.
1963   Billy became known as White House chaplain.
       Los Angeles campaign.
1966   London meetings.

1969	Neil Armstrong became the first man on the moon. Meetings held in Madison Square Garden. Richard Nixon became President and establishes church services in the White House.
1973	President Johnson died and Billy preached at his funeral.
1975	Ruth and Billy went to Taiwan for a series of evangelistic meetings and returned later that year.
1982	Billy preached in Moscow, the first time a Christian minister was allowed to preach there.
1983	Received Presidential Medal of Freedom.
1984	First official Evangelistic campaign in Russia.
1989	Berlin Wall came down.
1991	Soviet Union dissolved.
1992	Billy is diagnosed with Parkinson's Disease. He returned to Russia for a full-scale evangelistic mission.
1993	World Trade Center attacked.
1996	President Bill Clinton presented Billy and Ruth with the Congressional Gold Medal.
2001	Billy addressed the American nation, in the National Cathedral, after the September 11 terrorist attack.
2005	Travelled to New York for what he said would be his final evangelistic campaign.
2006	Still preaching the gospel of Christ.... The Celebration of Hope at New Orleans.

CHRISTIAN FOCUS PUBLICATIONS

Christian Focus | Christian Heritage | CF4K | Mentor

Christian Focus Publications publishes books for adults and children under its four main imprints: Christian Focus, Christian Heritage, CF4K and Mentor. Our books reflect that God's word is reliable and Jesus is the way to know him, and live for ever with him.

Our children's publication list includes a Sunday school curriculum that covers pre-school to early teens; puzzle and activity books. We also publish personal and family devotional titles, biographies and inspirational stories that children will love.

If you are looking for quality Bible teaching for children then we have an excellent range of Bible story and age specific theological books.

From pre-school to teenage fiction, we have it covered!

Find us at our web page:
www.christianfocus.com